SURFING THE PSYCHIC INTERNET

Copyright 2006
Daz Smith

All rights reserved. No part of this publication can be reproduced, stored in a retrieval system, or transmitted in any form or by any means, electronic, mechanical, photocopying, recording or otherwise, without the prior permission of the publishers and/or authors.

While every precaution has been taken in the preparation of this book, the publisher assumes no responsibilities for errors or omissions, or for damages resulting from the use of information contained herein.

Cover design by Daz Smith

ISBN: 978-1-4303-0940-6

For further information:

www.Arcanumbooks.co.uk
147 the Oval, Bath, BA2 2HF, U.K.

*For my mother who showed me that we could fly
& for Brenda who likes to fly with me!*

CONTENTS

Introduction 1
Welcome to the Matrix 5
Psychic Tools for Psychic Travel 7
Psychics & Portals 13
The Angels 19
Expansion 25
The Cycle of Knowledge 31
A Dark Intrusion 35
I See Dead People 43
Frequencies and Tingles. 49
The Universe has Many Voices. 53
A Warning 57
Knowledge of the Coming... 59
The Dark Ones Circle 63
Amethyst Gels 67
Changes 71
The Human Chakra System 79
A Watcher 81
A Psychic Warrior 85
Ripples, Waves and Secrets 91
Things to Come – Conflict and Hope! 97
Things To Come – Dark Revelations 109
Things to Come – Balance in Everything 123
A New World 139
YOU Can Travel The Psychic Internet 143
Meditation 145
How to Explore the Psychic Internet. 149
Surfing The Psychic Internet – You are not Alone! ... 157
About the Author 159

INTRODUCTION

The important thing is not to stop questioning. Curiosity has its own reason for existing. One cannot help but be in awe when he contemplates the mysteries of eternity, of life, of the marvellous structure of reality. It is enough if one tries merely to comprehend a little of this mystery every day.
Never lose a holy curiosity.
- **Albert Einstein** *(1879 - 1955)*

If you are now one of the millions who use the internet, you generally go to Google, you type in a question, hit the search button and back comes thousands of websites that hopefully hold your answer. What I do as a psychic explorer is calm my mind, ask a question and then through psychic travel I am transported through time and space to the answers within the psychic internet.

It's my belief that the popularity of the internet we all know and use, and the way it has touched those who use it is because it's the closest man can physically create to the generally unseen psychic internet that has existed around us all for millennia.

For thousands of years myths have existed about the Hall of Records, or the Akashic records, where information on everything that has ever happened is stored. Many people after near death experiences detail a vision of their life shown to them in pure detail in the span of a few brief seconds. Remote viewers or specially trained psychics can access information about anything, anywhere in time and space. All this leads to the psychic internet. A connection of interwoven dimensions hidden from man's everyday vision but open to his calm, psychic mind.

This book is about explorations within this psychic internet. We opened up our own Google-type portal, asked our questions and were whisked along time and space to a multitude of dimensions, life forms and to an understanding of man's place in the order of the universe.

This book is about finding a path to a greater spiritual understanding of yourself. By reading this, you are opening a doorway that will also allow YOU to experience and travel to far off places and to experience amazing new worlds and diverse life forms.

When I first started this psychic travelling I never imagined where it would lead, what would happen and whom I would meet. Each experience has allowed me to

Introduction

gradually piece together a cosmic jigsaw of questions that we all ask in our day-to-day lives, questions that define who we are and what our life is really about!

Chapter by chapter I will take you through some of the experiences I have had whilst in a small psychic circle group. This group consisted of mostly no more than four advanced psychic students at any one time who 'knew the psychic ropes' as they say, they were comfortable with each other and were open to new experiences. This group has gathered for well over twelve years and still meets to this day in the warmth of Brenda's tutelage. The main aim was personal spiritual development, but more excitingly, psychic exploration. All the group members were well acquainted with all manners of psychic methods and training. Many of our combined skills included; Clairvoyance, Mediumship, Telepathy, Channeling, Aura reading, Healing, Tarot & Divination tools, Meditation and Remote Viewing. Most of the psychics that came and went within the small group over the years were a little maverick, with most of us developing new methods of Psychic ability and an insatiable need to advance psychic theories, but most of all for pushing the boundaries and we did so on so many occasions!

At the end of this book we break down the Psychic processes and methods that we have used and developed over time into manageable sections that you can then use as a guide, either alone or as part of a small group, for your own psychic explorations. This form of psychic exploration is based around meditation and the visualisation of a portal which allows access to hyperspace and dimensions all around us. This can be just for spiritual progress, for information and for enjoyment. If there are any life questions you need answers for, they are both 'out there' and 'within you', YOU just need to open this portal to find them.

WELCOME TO THE MATRIX

The Matrix (1999)

Morpheus:

"You can take the blue pill and the story ends. You wake in your bed and you believe whatever you want to believe. You take the red pill and you stay in wonderland and I show you how deep the rabbit-hole goes. Remember that all I am offering is the truth. Nothing more".

This is exactly the same scenario that I was presented with when Brenda approached me after psychic development class one wet Wednesday evening. "Daz we have a small psychic circle group that meets up once a fortnight, it's usually four, but we're down to three now, we'd be pleased if you'd join us?" Without much thought and without actually knowing what a home circle group did, I found myself saying YES.

Now I look back and see how that one single decision took me on a fantastic journey of discovery across time and space. It allowed me to converse with a multitude of life forms that can only be described as alien, and at the same time, godlike. I was launched on a journey of self exploration allowing me to change, adapt, accept new forms of thinking, and also realise the truth about the parts we play in God's universal playground. A truth about how we as human beings have something that sets us apart from others in the multi-verses we interact with, a series of secrets that most of us have lost over the ages of time.

This book is a journey. It has no beginning, no middle and no end, because it's not over yet, and I now realise it never will be. It's about my communications and journeys in the hyperspace that surrounds us all. It's a guide for others to follow into this unexplored metropolis of diverse life, and a pathway to understanding the true meaning of who we are and our place in the universe.

PSYCHIC TOOLS FOR PSYCHIC TRAVEL

We have found a strange footprint on the shores of the unknown. We have devised profound theories, one after another, to account for its origins. At last, we have succeeded in reconstructing the creature that made the footprint And lo! It is our own.
- Sir Arthur Eddington (1882 - 1944)

We meet like many thousands of other groups around the world, around the universe. We sit in a quiet place, calm our minds, and interlink in a living chain of pulsating energy, we free the soul from the body then explore the hyperspace and dimensions around us.

'The Group' has been going for over twelve years and my participation has been for most of these. We are generally between three and four members in size, though we do have people that migrate in and out of the group, replaced by new intriguing minds when the time feels right. Brenda is the group leader, a tall, wise and graceful woman, who by her own admission, has led a colourful life, that has at times been hard. Brenda has the air of a schoolteacher, long flowing grey hair and glasses that focus the glow from her eyes. She doesn't mince her words; she's to the point, love it or leave it, but always truthful with a yearning to explore and to know more.

For more years than I can count, Brenda has taught generations of inquisitive minds at the local Spiritualist church the techniques of spiritual and psychic exploration. I was originally one of her many students, I still am, and at times she is now one of mine.

The circle group takes the format passed down from medium to medium and other occult practitioners for many thousands of years. The circle is believed to be a magical symbol, its strength and power is believed to come from its encompassing shape. I do believe the old tales about the power of shapes and the circular form, but I also believe its use goes deeper than this and that the circular shape itself enhances the flow of energy needed to explore.

During deep meditations, energy from within the group members dissipates from the body and moves in the form of a gentle mist. Generally the energy has a light luminescence and glows in the darkness. It moves with a purpose, mingling with the energy from the other group members, all swirling in a clockwise rotational movement. Slowly at first until a deep state is reached, then when the four of us resonate at a unified frequency – a single silent note - it picks up speed to a dizzying spinning wall of protective energy, which becomes our barrier between us and the shadows - a protective circle.

With every exploration of the consciousness there are as many dangers as everyday life, with this in mind it's essential that a protective format be used to stop or hinder any unfriendly life forms. These we call 'The Shadows'. They sit on the edge of our knowing, moving in the fringes of where our consciousness can just make out their forms. Some were once human, others are lost, ancient souls, looking and longing, but drawn towards the light, life and love. There are others that have intent, deceivers who want the one thing they can't have in hyperspace, all the experiences of a real body - touch, feeling and human sensations. The protection is simple, it always has been. LOVE, love in the form of a radiant white living energy, reaching out from inside you. A mental projection of this energy forming a barrier around oneself is a simple form of protection. What we build around us every session is a living wall of impenetrable love, will and intent. A living barrier, allowing the body to be left silent, but guarded as other parts of the whole - travel. I believe this mystical shape - the circle, stimulates the flow of the energy matrix and the synchronisation of the group in to a consolidated rhythm. A single, silent note.

We also use a single centrally located candle. We have experimented with other sources of light, but it's our belief that the electromagnetic emissions from electric lights can hinder any perceived imagery, and negate results from our experiences. Why do we need a light you ask? During each session we periodically break free at key points, and in the dim light hastily record notes and observations.

The four cardinal points of the compass also seem very important to the performance of this group. With guidance we have been placed within these points, and I feel this is with relevance to the energy emissions from the individuals during a session, and how these interact with the space and energy around us. If any of us move to a different cardinal point, then the session and results change. The flow of energy is shifted and it all needs time for re-adjustment. Any circle groups using this as a guide may note that constantly changing members and seating positions will vary the results and hinder a build up of an energy pattern over time.

The last tool we use for the sessions, the most important elements in the process - ourselves. We try to be relaxed, clear headed, not hungry, but also not full of food and drink. Loose clothing is essential as well as a very open mind.

When I close my eyes with the intent of a hyperspace experience, my body instantly picks up on this and now automatically starts a shutdown of all unnecessary processes. Breathing slows, it becomes deep and drawn out. Each breath takes the muscles of the body into a lower and lower state of deep relaxation.

Breathing is now so deep I can hardly feel it. My true mind is now stirring as the physical body shuts down and allows it some freedom. Usually at this point I initiate a grounding ritual for myself. This is a process purely to let the travelling parts of me know the way home. Like an organic internal homing beacon and combined autopilot. If you need to pull out quickly you will always get home. Sometimes a little shaken – but generally safe.

My personal process of grounding involves me imagining or creating long sharp pointed spears of matter, which shoot out from my feet at great speed, deep into the ground beneath me. Like the deep penetrating roots of a tree.

The last tool in place, my heartbeat slowing, the breathing gets deeper, then deeper, all sensation of the physical body slowly starts to fade, the chair fades, and the room and then finally, you're free.

PSYCHICS & PORTALS

The real voyage of discovery consists not in seeking new landscapes but in having new eyes.
*- **Marcel Proust** (1871 - 1922)*

The four of us sit in our usual places, the cardinal points of the compass. There's Brenda to the left, Jane to the right and Karen across from me.

Brenda is the oldest. A spiritual teacher, we have all at some point or another been one of Brenda's students. She now teaches generation after generation of people how to open up to the world around them from the backrooms of the local Spiritualist Church.

Jane has been part of the group for a year now. A strong, fiercely independent woman, she is always on the go and always learning a new skill - Reiki, Hypnosis, Meditation and just about anything she can use to equip her on her long journey ahead.

Karen feels like the baby of the group. Young and so full of life with a caring smile, we often feel like we take her under our wing as she opens up to these new worlds, experiences and horizons. She's sometimes fearful, often naïve, but always curious.

This leaves me, Daz, an addict to all things paranormal from an early age. Once, one of Brenda's many students in the art of Clairvoyance and Mediumship. Now years later I repay the favour by teaching Brenda the art of Remote Viewing. But for now I was an integrated part of this evolving group of psychics, who for years had been probing the boundaries of hyperspace and the dimensions that envelops all.

We close our eyes and relax in the flickering light of a solitary, central candle located on a small wooden table in the middle of the small circle of chairs. Within a few silent pregnant minutes, a swirling mass of living, moving energy, wriggles as it grows out of the ground in front of us. Rotating, swirling and swaying as it reaches aloft towards the ceiling, and on up into the reaches beyond. This is our gateway, our vehicle, our portal. The portal grows with each moment, sucking in the energy that is built up around and between us, as it writhes like a cobra dancing to a flute. When the energy achieves a critical mass, elongated and deformed, tubular branches spring out from the trunk and reach out across time and space.

At the same time as all this is happening, a ring of white pulsating energy is spinning wildly clockwise around us until it reaches a crescendo, silent in the physical world, but in the meditation state, humming and vibrating with a solid, structured note. This is our ring of protection. A ring formed from our good intentions, years of training and the pulsating white life force that flows through us all.

Behind the group just out of reach, stepping out of the darkness and just visible in the dim light of the energy, are life forms. Human in shape, but large and with no discernable facial features, they radiate a warmth not often felt in man. They always watch, not intrusive nor instructive, just watching, neutral, observing and waiting. These are the fabled Angels of old.

I feel myself looking left and am aware that the other members of the group, one by one, enter the base of the swirling portal. Lifted up out of their seats they glide silently towards the swirling mass. After a momentary transformation of energy, they are swept along through the twisted living branches of energy, up and out into hyperspace.

It then becomes my turn to travel, and although my physical body sits still and silent in the chair, the rest of me, the real me, gently rises and moves into the bright pulsating portal.

As one enters this mass of living pulsating energy, a heavy viscous feeling momentarily impedes your movements. You feel a slight resistance at first, then a relaxing freedom as you break through it. Inside the portal the energy spirals upwards in a chaotic vortex, reaching up high, way past what was the ceiling up out into the unknown. With a mental acknowledgement, not unlike a gentle nod of acceptance, you are sucked and projected through a mass of spiraling vortices. Imagery that looks alien and vaguely recognizable fill your consciousness. Stars speed past streaking through the midnight blue, luminous clouds of gaseous matter, and spider web like tendrils of silver matter stretching out amongst dark openness and vast amounts of tumbling space and time.

The movement is chaotic, trying to focus on the imagery is impossible, fleeting glimpses tantalise and astound. Faces from the future and past, places, vibrant living colours, and indescribable sensations ripple through the mind. The whole experience is not unlike being a passenger in a roller coaster, you want to watch, to take it all in slowly, but the vehicle won't let you.

Landing is never a motion, it has no ending place, the experience just seems to dissipate rapidly and as you look around, it dawns on you that the ride is over. As they said in the classic film 'The wizard of Oz', "we're not in Kansas anymore Toto."

THE ANGELS

Psalm 91:11-12 "For He will give His angels charge of you, to guard you in all your ways."

During numerous sessions as individuals, and as the group, we have encountered some of these strange supernatural beings. We have been told many times by the communicating life forms that for protection the Archangels watch over the group and the work we do. As they do so with many others around the planet. With a little concentration they can be seen on the fringes of our protective circle. They are taller than humans, probably seven to eight feet tall, and surprisingly, against all the stories I've read, they appear to be dressed in black and not the expected white. They do have wings, these appear to be tinged with radiating yellow, glowing and soft, and blurred when looked at, not unlike the wings of a Hummingbird in flight. I'm told that this is a manifestation of their resonating vibrational frequency, which being a lot higher and therefore faster than ours, produces this blurred, luminescent glow. I can't tell if the wings have feathers, like the traditional Christian imagery, and when I have tried to focus and view this, I'm told quite sternly "this isn't really the point. The point is they exist, and they are there for the benefit of us all."

One thing I have noticed over time with our experiences with the Angels is that I can't see their faces. Sometimes their heads are bowed in concentration of their task, but generally their faces are purposely hidden from me. One time when I glanced at one during a deep meditation I asked "why can I not see your face?" I was told that this honour is reserved for those who really need it, people who have lost the way, the sick, the cold, the lonely, the needy. I was told that if you're one of those lucky few who have looked upon the face of an angel you must ask yourself why they have shown you, and that somewhere within the experience there is an important message there waiting for you to unlock.

Since time began, man has always reported beings not like us but tall, winged, glowing and pure, full of love, and with a gentle understanding of human traits and needs. The Bible details these beings as The Angels. Ministers of the will of God - the messengers. God bestowed upon angels great wisdom, freedom, and power. Their many appearances in the New Testament are an indication of their universal role - side by side with the development of man.

The Angels

These spiritual beings comprise the celestial court and are called Angels (from the Greek meaning "messenger") because, according to the Bible, they carry out missions at God's command. In order to complete these missions, they can at times assume bodily form. According to the Bible, their missions are at times of great importance. Angels are purely spiritual or bodiless persons, some of whom behold the face of God and thus are in bliss.

Archangels are generally taken to mean "chief" or "leading Angel" they are the most frequently mentioned throughout the Bible but can be found in Islam and Judaism. The Archangels have a unique role as God's messenger to the people at critical times in history and salvation as in The Annunciation and Apocalypse. The word Archangel comes from the Greek – first, or primary messenger.

Of special significance is Michael, as he has been invoked as patron and protector by the Church from the time of the Apostles. The Eastern Rite and many others, place him over all the Angels as Prince of the Seraphim. He is described as the "chief of princes" and as the leader of the forces of heaven in their triumph over Satan and his followers. Seraphim (plural of Seraph) are an order of angels with fervent zeal and religious ardour. They are described as having three pairs of wings, one of which covers their faces as a token of humility, one of which covers their feet as a token of respect and one of which allows them to fly.

The Angel Gabriel first appeared in the Old Testament in the prophesies of Daniel, he announced the prophecy of 70 weeks. He appeared to Zechariah to announce the birth of St. John the Baptist. It was also Gabriel which proclaimed the Annunciation of Mary to be the mother of the Lord and Saviour. In biblical tradition, he is sometimes regarded as the angel of death, the prince of fire and thunder, but more frequently as one of God's chief messengers, and traditionally said to be the only angel that can speak Syriac and Chaldee. In Islam, Gabriel is one of God's chief messengers but other above mentioned titles are not given to him *(for example the angel of death is Azrael)*.

The Angel Raphael first appeared in the book of Tobit. He announces "I am the Angel Raphael, one of the seven who stand before the throne of God." Regarding the healing powers attributed to Raphael, we have little more than his declaration to Tobit that he was sent by the Lord to heal him of his blindness and to deliver Sarah, his daughter-in-law, from the devil that was the serial killer of her husbands.

Uriel is often identified as the cherub who "stands at the Gate of Eden with a fiery sword," or as the angel who "watches over thunder and terror". Uriel is identified variously as a seraph, cherub, regent of the sun, flame of God, angel of the Divine Presence, archangel of salvation, and, in later scriptures, identified with the "face of God". He is often depicted carrying a book or a papyrus scroll (for his wisdom). Uriel is a patron of the Arts, and described by Milton as the "sharpest sighted spirit in all of Heaven."

The group has at times been blessed by the guiding presence of the four key messengers, Gabriel, Michael, Raphael and Uriel. Standing at a distance, but close enough to matter, they protect and guide, they seem to hold back the darkness with the glow from their outstretched wings as they stand at four points behind us. Sometimes they themselves guide us with cryptic messages, informing on new uncharted pathways and teachings. When I think back to them I find it hard to place them within our order of contacts and communication, as not only are they kind, angelic, soft and impacting on the human soul, but from terrible stories told in the Christian Bible, they are God's right hand men, His holy messengers, but also His dogs of war. I deeply wonder what goes on inside the mind of a life form so devoted, so spiritual, so inspiring, but also knowing that they are the instruments of destruction in their obedience to their lord. Maybe one day I'll ask one, or maybe you'll do it for me.

EXPANSION

Experience is not what happens to a man; it is what a man does with what happens to him.
*- **Aldous Huxley** (1894 - 1963)*

The psychic group sessions could never come around fast enough for me. For the few days before the next meeting I could feel my senses grow in anticipation. I find that like a drug, the body starts to crave the sensations and states caused by our travels in time and space, and mine lets me know with intense mood swings. Mainly these came about if a session had to be cancelled, and like a junkie, I would slip into a state of psychic cold turkey. But this time I did not have to battle with my internal demons as it was Friday and I was sitting on the soft leather couch, one of a group of four, all of us slipping slowly into uncharted realms.

The expanse of space opened up before me in a sharp intense flash of white light. Following this started the darting, racing through one of the tendril like branches of the portal. Stars, clouds of intense, vibrant colour and large patches of cold blue space wind their way in and out of every part of my vision, twisting and turning in a nauseating rhythm as they slip past the corners of my vision. I try to turn my head to focus and stop to watch the glorious spectacle in detail, but this is in vain as the mechanism takes hold and projects me faster towards my final destination. Then I'm there! But it's not a gradual slow down to a stop like any physical movement. It's a, your moving fast, spiraling, turning, straining to see the amazing imagery passing before you. Then you're there. No feeling of a transference or deceleration, just one state or place to another.

I look all around me, more with my sense than with my physical eyes. The whole being or part of you that travels senses everything. You can see, hear and sense from every angle. A little like having eyes that can see 360 degrees around except you're not using your eyes. Generally I find that I sense life forms first, and then as they move to approximately twenty feet away, I start to see them form into detail and shape.

As I look around I feel a huge amount of dense dark space. I momentarily feel alone and vulnerable as my senses reach out into the darkness and move away from me at speed whilst looking back towards myself showing me how small I am in this vast expanse of darkness. Then with a shift of attention, my senses and vision are back again waiting for the lessons to start.

Expansion

After a small space of time, I sense a movement out in front of me and to the left. Slowly out of the darkness a luminescent form moves towards me with a graceful, caressing movement, almost as if the space itself were hindering it, like our slow cumbersome movement through water. The form came closer, and unusually as it did, it took no real structured form. When it was no more than six feet in front of me, I could see it clearly. A white, cloudy moving form like a jellyfish made of smoke. Small sparkling lights pulsated and moved within the folds of the cloud as it rippled and waved like it felt the movement of a cosmic wind. The winding tracks of sparkles followed invisible tracks up and over the shape mixing in between and behind moving folds of semi transparent material.

I brought my focus back from looking at the strange life form in front of me and inside my head sarcastically asked "well what now?" I immediately heard a reply, deep, and full of a vibration, "we would like to try an experiment." The voice was in my head, but at the same time, focused all around me, clear, concise, and also reassuring. I felt no concerns and no feelings of revulsion or fear, and yet a strange life form with no real shape, and no features had just communicated with me. Now when I look back I feel it's the whole experience that allows part of you to be so finely attuned, that intent good or bad, radiates from all life forms in clear discernable patterns like a detectable aura that precedes all life forms as they move.

"What do you want to do?" I asked the form curiously.
"We want to meet within you, to become part of you, to experience you" came the reply. At first I didn't know how to respond, and a quick succession of scenarios played through my mind. For an instant, fear and adrenalin kicked in, and my pulse raced as wild imagery of becoming permanently possessed by "the jelly being from Mars" took shape and form. I pushed hard moving these obstructions to one side and responded "Okay, let's give it a try."

I sensed an affirmation from the floating mass of spectral energy in front of me, and after a slight pause it moved slowly but consciously towards me. Prickly sensations surged over the entire front of my body, except it wasn't my body as I wasn't really there. I could feel a slight tickling sensation, not unlike a breeze against bare skin. The life form continuously moved forwards and internally a pressure formed deep inside as my heart quickened with my realisation of "shit, this is really happening!" By now adrenalin had naturally pumped around my physical body in reaction to the event, and for a brief minute keeping the event on course and not aborting in panic were the only thoughts racing and battling for dominance inside my head. These passed, and with them, the realisation that the life form was not in front of me anymore but inside of me.

I could feel it, it was probing and exploring within me. It felt like a little part of the space in my head where thoughts form had been numbed, like when at the dentist, and within the numbness I could feel the inquisitive probing from the life form. It couldn't understand the qualities of vision, and my wonderment at its wonderment stirred emotions that it found pleasing and also perplexing. I could feel the struggle of a life form trying to understand a completely alien environment in every way to theirs. I explored in wonderment the alien. As it learnt about us I also learnt. The life form for example did not construct emotions like us. It had emotional reactions, but the response and effects of emotions are much less, almost dampened. It felt love and pain but in a more controlled manner causing no extreme response to unforeseen circumstances.

We stayed like this for some minutes two beings entwined as one, learning and probing, creating new sensations and changing both of our paradigms forever. Then with a shift and a sensation of breaking away from an energy source, the life form slowly left. Like a warming glow I could feel the numb area return to glowing life as the energy shifted away. The life form floated to a position a few feet away from me. We exchanged a mutual thank you even though nothing was spoken, like the experience had generated a mutual respect for the differences in us both.

From behind me I could feel the portal open and the uncontrollable pull of the event ending, and the long slow return to consciousness start, it's by now an almost mechanical procedure. Ten minutes later I was back, comfortably sunken in to the deep folds of Brenda's leather couch.

I wanted to recount this experience for you travelers, as a guide to understanding what a process of communication may feel like. By overcoming the initial human fear, and by flowing with the experience instead of fighting it, we can all use and learn from these experiences. I personally feel that the life form and I both gained from the sharing of the same space and what seems like a one-way situation of another life form inhabiting you can turn out to be something much, much more.

THE CYCLE OF KNOWLEDGE

To be conscious that you are ignorant is a great step to knowledge.
- ***Benjamin Disraeli (1804 - 1881)***

For the next three meetings I was shown and I experimented with what can only be termed as 'mind movement exercises'. The usual warm down procedures took place, where the bodily functions are gradually slowed and kept to a minimum. The weird observation about this process is that the functions important to life like heart rate and breathing, slow almost to a stop and everything feels as though it has been suspended in time, Yet the basic senses - smell, sight and hearing are enhanced. Even though the eyes are closed in meditation, you feel you can see more clearly. The visions that manifest from the subconscious feel vivid and crystal in their clarity and form.

After I had reached a deep state of consciousness the lesson began. I was to take my essence, my consciousness and move it to a corner of the room near the ceiling, and observe and record the view from there in minute detail. Then the invisible teacher would have me move myself into and through different objects to experience the physical feeling of the process. One of the main lessons was to understand that I could fit 'me' within a few atoms, and still there would be so much space that the horizon goes on forever. There is no such thing as space, there is just everything.

These lessons grew in intensity over the following weeks; the movements became faster and more distant. Distance is of no object when in these states of consciousness, the end of the universe is a heartbeat away, and a space just a breath away can feel like an expanse with no boundaries.

Some of the strangest feelings I experienced at this stage were from movements into and through everyday objects of, glass, metal, and wood. Once a movement exercise through a wooden stairs banister left me with an overbearing smell of fresh sawdust, but the actual trip was gentle as the movement took the form of the fibers as we swayed left and right as I moved through the fibrous matter of the wooden banister. The banister itself only a matter of inches in diameter took some minutes to transgress. A definite example of the implicate nature of the universe as referred to in the immortal words of William Blake:

'To see a World in a Grain of Sand, And Heaven in a Wild Flower. Hold Infinity in the palm of your hand, And Eternity in an hour'

These exercises were a part of training to allow me to travel anywhere within a moments thought. It was to allow me to travel without the conscious mind stepping in and saying "whoa, you can't do this – it can't be done". One of the biggest obstacles to the secret of man is the conscious mind, its doubts, its fears, and its reasoning. It takes many years of training to quiet the conscious mind, to blend it into the background and allow the true possibilities of man to shine through. Only the repetitive nature of teaching and learning can undo these unseen, but binding, chains that limit man's true potential.

The repetitive nature of the teachings imposed on me is found through all teaching practices throughout our every day lives – the student practices until he gets it right, then he moves onto a new lesson. It has been explained to us that this is the same pattern throughout the universe; it is the cycle of knowledge. Every student especially those who enter the realms of esoteric studies will be taught this way, but as one student to another, when you reach a time when the lesson seems to repeat and a plateau has been reached, don't give up. Take up the challenge, follow through with the teachings, observe, learn, and remember, but never, never give in. You're close, closer than you could possibly know.

A DARK INTRUSION

Some things have to be believed to be seen.
*- **Ralph Hodgson**, on ESP*

The group was going well. Each of us travelled our way through the universe through the winding branches of the portal. Within a session we would all report on fascinating life forms and observations of far off places, mainly returning and grasping for the vocabulary to describe what we had experienced. Sometimes, though not often, the experiences overlapped and what I had experienced coincided with impressions from one of the other members of our circle.

The evening started well. Before we started our usual cool down, we exchanged gossip about our busy lives and joked at some of the rising concerns in the world. We all felt that the group was progressing, along which pathway we did not know, but the lessons and combined experiences leant towards a general enlightening, an education like no other. As well as the growing confidence in what we were shown, also grew a sense of watching darkness. A heavy unsure feeling always lurking far in the background, sometimes moving too close and momentarily coming into the field of our vision like the fleeting movement in the corner of your eye. You saw it but what was it, did you really see it. Tonight I would see it.

I folded into the vacuum of the portal as it sucked me headlong up and out into colorful horizons of spider web like stars and clouds of luminescent gases. I could feel no part of my physical body as I sped at tremendous speed through the spiraling tubes towards a hidden destination.

Touchdown! Instantly the name Mars entered my mind as my vision was filled with a red filtered landscape of a dry, harsh looking world. All around me I could see and sense dense formations of rock that penetrated the surface and was met everywhere by a thick dense sand or dust. A sudden rush as if being pulled backwards at great speed and seeing the scene before you stretch with you as you go, and I was moved to a new location but on the same planet.

Before me lay an open plain, less craggy than the one before. Towering out of the thick red earth in front of me was an ancient structured form, a structure dominating the landscape, but also in some way fitting in with it. I looked up to where the sides met at an apex and recognised the familiar shape of a pyramid. Thick red dust covered the form and flowed across the base in large rolling dunes. In awe I could have stayed and watched for millennia, probably as long as it had been there, but this was not to be as an unseen force pulled me from behind, from this vision back into the darkness of space.

Time seemed to last for minutes as I desperately tried to hold on to the vision of the red planet as it stretched away from me and was replaced by the vibrant animated imagery of portal travel.

I landed again, this time I could feel my non-physical feet hit the surface with a soft cushioned feeling. Looking around the contrast was amazing. Where as before the colour was a hazy red, I was now in a bright place filled with heavy blacks and seas of rolling grey landscapes. I knew right away that this had to be the moon. We had all seen it on TV as astronauts bounced like kids in play. I turned to my left gawping at the harsh contours - and found it. Rising out from behind a small cluster of rocks was a pyramid structure. It looked a little more worn by the ravages of time than the first, but it was unmistakingly a pyramid. It gleamed grey, cold in colour but majestic in form. The edges were worn and in places broken. It too was in a plateau, allowing generous amount of space between it and the surrounding rocky landscapes. I was farther from this structure than the previous one, but it could have been the same size, it's hard to be sure. I sensed a feeling of time and of millennia, but again it's hard to be sure - the environment is so harsh. I could have sat and watched for an age. I followed the edges up to the top and back down the opposite side. I looked at the shape as a whole noting the difference in colour as one edge moved into a dark shadow away from me.

As quick as this vision had started, I was whisked sideways with a jolt that made my vision stream and the image of the pyramid seemed to stretch out as I hurtled across space. Almost instantaneously I was in another harsh landscape. Almost immediately the colour of the light provided by the deep blue sky above reassured me that I was again back home. Towering before me almost perched perfectly under the hot tingling sun was one of the Egyptian pyramids, dusty, battered but majestic. The size seemed similar to the moon pyramid but both smaller than the Martian structure. I was standing on a raised plateau a few hundred metres away from the monolithic structure that radiated nobility. Far behind the structure, clouds of dust were dancing on the crest of sand dunes as the wind played on the edges and down into the rolling curves. One thing that entered my mind after seeing all three imposing structures was the location. All were situated within landscapes of dust and a sterile isolation. The feelings this generated were of a planned intention to the placement, one I was just about to question when the pulling started and increased at speed until I was pulled or vacuumed back to Brenda's living room and the circle group.

I quietly spent minutes in the darkness of my solitude thinking over the journey and the unforgettable presence the structures had imparted within me. And like every man when facing new experiences, questions raced in to the forefront of my mind, yearning for answers, answers I knew would not be forthcoming.

Slowly the question faded into memory as the expanse of meditative black filled my consciousness expanding my internal vision. It was then that I noticed them. A slight movement or ripple in the energy patterns to the left of me focused my attention. I looked hard, not with eyes but a vision more acute, the internal vision of sight, sense and feeling all combined. Nothing, I could see nothing but the blackness of my own conscious state. I watched silently, on edge, senses radiating from me like an invisible radar sending waves rippling out across the room and space and time itself. But nothing stirred. I relaxed and was just turning back to my meditation when it came again, a swift movement from the centre of our circle. The very place we thought was impenetrable and safe. From out of the floor in front of us two gaseous shapes grew, winding, hissing and forming into loose shapes of men clothed in ragged black, hooded but with no features. From under the ripped floating tendril of black were twisted disfigured limbs shaped into long clawed fingers. The two creatures formed in front of me as I watched, stunned by the fact that the protective circle was broken. Then they came. Forward they pounced in a movement so recognisably predatorial. Leaping, with a great speed and with a gentle gliding motion, towards me, its arms reaching, clawing, wanting me. What happened next is a blur. As the first creature reached me I remember spinning and a light spinning past my vision as I rolled to the left. Two severed hands from the creature span past me and out of sight. The second creature had now jumped past where I once sat, turned, looked with a low stooping stare and leapt again. I span again and felt my arms arc as a beam of radiant light shot upward with my motion. Spinning as I landed I saw the second creature land awkwardly beside its companion. Both looked at their limbless arms, then at me as they started to shrink and dissipate in the same way they had formed. I watched, stunned and confused until the black gas had completely vanished and a stillness filled the air. I looked down and in my right hand lay a sword brightly twinkling in the light from the candle.

A Dark Intrusion

How and why I managed to slay those creatures still fascinates me. After analysing the experience I know that my reactions were autonomous and instinctive. I had reacted to the situation in a way that flowed from deep inside – a hidden but unlocked new part of me. One of the questions that still haunts me, with no answers, is how did they get there. A protective circle established by four competent psychic explorers, a technique used successfully for thousands of years – and yet broken, and for what?

We discussed this experience in the hours after we had all returned from our travel, and as the others recounted their happenings in the zone, I had the nagging feeling that this would not be the last we would see of the dark ones.

I SEE DEAD PEOPLE

For certain is death for the born. And certain is birth for the dead; Therefore over the inevitable. Thou shouldst not grieve.
- ***Bhagavad Gita*** *(250 BC - 250 AD), Chapter 2*

The four of us arrived at Brenda's one by one and found our way to the usual positions, mine I feel being the best as I had a prime position on the comfortable leather sofa, brown and squeaky, but warm and soft and it molded to my shape within minutes. Comfort is a key part of any psychic process, the body needs to be totally free and relaxed.

Brenda was to my left and the other two group members, Jane and Karen, sat to my right forming a rough outline of a circle. Karen lit a candle positioned on a table in the middle of the circle and its warming blanket of yellow light sparkled through the water each of us had in small glasses – just in case the session got hot or uncomfortable. We settled back in our seats and individually started our cool down processes. This trigger for me instantly relaxes my muscles and with the next breath out my shoulders drop what feels like eight inches and my body starts to react to its familiar pattern of deep meditation. After ten minutes I unusually have the distinct urge to look up towards the group. Not to look with physical eyes but with my senses. Before me out of the darkness, formed thick columns of energetic light where my friends were sitting. Encased in this light, it eminates as though evaporating off them, and the farther from the body it escaped, the more it dissipated until it disappeared high above our heads. Each column had a mixture of layered tones and hues but overall the effect from each was a majority of one colour. Brenda's to my left was yellow and orange; Jane radiated deep reds to pink, and Karen soft purples to deep blues. The effect where the fringes touched from all four of us danced above our heads like a miniature etheric living aurora borealis.

My attention shifted to a movement in my peripheral vision just at the corner of my eye. Looking to the right I saw small concentrated white balls of light slowly bob and weave as they moved from the fringes of darkness towards us and the light that now filled the room. That first light I followed as it moved closer. When it reached the edge of the circle I could see it change form almost with a little concentration like squinting, the faint outline of a young girl took shape as the form moved in a soft, slow movement. The other lights which were all around us by now, had also changed form into people – people everywhere all of varying sizes and shapes. It's like a switch, the moment the mind accepts what it sees then they just form into place like a light switch going on and whoa! – A room full of people.

The next impression that flooded through me at seeing these life forms is of pain. Not mine but the overbearing sense of pain and despair from the visitors permeating the space around us. On looking closely, this pain could also be seen in the sad, transparent looks upon their faces. Fleeting distant memories swamp the space around us as the thoughts and feelings of families lost flitter amongst the energies like etheric butterflies in flight. One of the life forms moves closer. It's the form of the young girl. I can see the resemblance of a smile flicker for a second and catch a sense of her fascination of us in our state of being alive, of being human. After some minutes of life forms coming close to the circle members, almost as if basking in the warmth of the energies and radiant light, I asked the girl if she would like to experience life through me as she had in the past. With a very eager nod of her head she agrees. I acknowledged her response, closed my vision and immediately started my decent into an even lower state of mind.

Long minutes passed, and with each deep breath I could feel part of me shift to an area deep inside and a space expanded where the life form would enter. This experience isn't much different to a bubble expanding within, creating a space as parts of me are pushed into other spaces. A few minutes later the process begins as the girl slowly moves towards me.

With our energy fields touching my pulse rate skyrockets, and a sensation akin to hair standing up on the back of my neck envelopes my whole form. Slowly I feel the form enter me deeply, high up near the top of my crown. As this happens a part of me is shifted or pulled into a strange space. This space is like no other I have experienced, it's as if time has stood still and I'm in a dark enclosed box, neither in my body but not entirely out of my body, just in a different place within it. I could sense the girl's elation at feeling form and density, and could feel her joy when she moved my physical eyes up and down against the back of my eyelids. She looked around the room using her newfound physical senses, and this thrilled her as she saw the colours of the life forms dance and glide amongst the radiant tendrils of etheric energy.

After some time, I don't know how long, it was time for us to separate and I could feel the irresistible pull backward into my form and the conscious need for me to expand and fill my form once more, grew in anticipation like a deep thirst.

When back in my body I could once again see the room around me. The overall feeling had changed, the despair was still there but was now being slowly replaced by a sense of hope and of universal love. Everyone in the room including the circle exchanged gifts, gifts of knowledge and gifts of respect, and most of all gifts of pure love.

The forms retreated away from the circle gliding past Brenda's shoulders in a haunting flowing movement into the darkness beyond. The little girl turned in mid flow of movement looked back at me and acknowledged a silent thank you and smiled. Then with a movement back towards the darkness she quickly disappeared in a sparkle of intense white light. The session was over. I shrugged as the light in the room slowly faded to its darkness and I began the struggle from this place where anything is possible to back home, back to a physical limited form.

On reflection, I felt that the forms we attracted with our light that day, needing something from us, something they couldn't get anywhere else - a connection with the physical world and a connection with the memories of all that was once real for them.

The energy created by a meditation circle acts like a beacon in the darkness. It draws all life forms to it good, bad and sometimes, the ugly. In this case the interaction between these forms and us helped them accept and remember certain truths and hence benefited us all. I learnt about them, the lost, and the forgotten. Missing souls yearning for the past and lost in the vacuum this creates. If you on your hyperspace travels meet souls like these, be kind, guide them, and most of all learn from them – life is the journey and sometimes we all take the wrong path and need directions from a stranger.

FREQUENCIES AND TINGLES.

After silence, that which comes nearest to expressing the inexpressible is music.
*- **Aldous Huxley** (1894 - 1963)*

The circle group was in mid session. The experience so far had gone well and I was in a state of movement into a deeper state of consciousness. Before me I saw a 'helper'. A being that appeared from nowhere in mid flow of walking. Don't ask how, but during these experiences the male, female essence of a life form is instantly and silently communicated – and this life form was male.

Stride after stride he moved across the space towards me. Amazed I asked how he had just appeared from nowhere and was told. "It was the frequency at which they were formed. It was different from my present one but with a little self adjustment they could alter it to a frequency more harmonious with ours and then we could see them." He also explained that they were always around us, always close to us but that we just couldn't see them, that our physical eyes were too primitive and not sensitive enough - most of the time.

The helper then explained he was here to expand and help me with the techniques know as 'Phasing'. This was advanced movement in altered states allowing access to remote places through a relaxed state of mind. Phasing, he said, was the progression from one state or place to another with no starting, stopping or inertia. The mind controls this; the mind is the navigation and has access to anything, anywhere'. He then suggested that together we try some of these movements to get me started.

The helper proceeded to instruct me on how all of this was achieved using the mind, and I felt almost hypnotised by the soft flowing tone of his voice as he finished the explanation and motioned for me to try. So I tried.

The weird thing is that when the exercise starts it really does feel like real 'physical' movement. I noticed a definite shifting not unlike a lagging sensation or pulling. It's like, not all of you reaches a destination at the same time and a fraction of a second later, part of you follows like an elastic band stretching towards a point in time and the rear of the band will get there a fraction later. This pulling can be felt primarily around the face, especially the cheekbones and eyes. These areas seem to have sensory receptors that sense hyperspacial movement and activity more than the rest of the body. I have felt the ripples of an approaching life form in hyperspace as tingle sensations here more than any other part of my body. Maybe you can use this as a guide in your travels too.

The helper described to me how the face was one big receptor of information, and that the eyes, cheeks, nose and every part of the face was important when interpreting the various environments. "You don't need your eyes to see" he said.

The helper then pointed to the other group members with a sweep of his arm. Before me they appeared out of the void and I could see their forms glowing with a radiant animated light in the darkness, Brenda to the left, Karen opposite and Jane to the right of me. "This is why you work as a group. Individually you all have separate resonating frequencies. These form to create unique sounds and notes. When we work together in groups these notes join together and the frequencies become like chords, a beautiful form of music, spiritual and alive." As the helper explained this concept, he also showed it with visions of the group represented by different shapes, a square, a circle, a triangle and hexagon, of which each of these were in a different colour. Then when he mentioned 'as a group' the shapes all spun in a large fast circle creating a luminous wheel of glowing rainbow colours, coupled with a hum not unlike a Buddhist chant that got louder as the spinning got faster. The shapes, not discernable now as they were, were replaced by a spinning wheel of light and sound, and I felt that he knew the message was learnt – and learnt well as I could feel him radiate the energy of a smile and a mixed air of satisfaction.

Nearing the end of this lesson the helper detailed how this knowledge needed to be written down. He was showing me, explaining the subtleties so that a book could be written for others to use as a guide to follow and explore their heritage, their birthright. "Write everything" he said, "It's all important – the little details more than anything."

As he appeared - the helper left. They don't seem to waste time with the little courtesies of 'real life', I have yet to have an experience where time is wasted saying "hello" or "goodbye", they just know when the time is over, and gently leave. And this is what he did. He turned and walked away and as he strode he vanished mid step, fading into the darkness, into another place. A second later and I too had to leave as I spiralled awkwardly backwards, towards my physical waking and physical consciousness.

THE UNIVERSE HAS MANY VOICES.

"What is God?" I asked.
"You are God"
"Does God exist?" I replied.
"Do you exist?"
Dialogue with a dimensional life form. *– Feb 2000*

Whatever the scientists and experts tell you, or whatever you read in books and the fabricated, shrink-wrapped, tabloid press, do not believe any of them. The universe is teeming with life; it exudes from every crevice, every nook and cranny. The problem is seeing it, and most people have a hard time believing anything they cannot see with their physical eyes. You need to look with better eyes than the ones we use for our everyday life; you have to look with the eyes of the soul. When you do, you will see distant horizons filled with unrealized dreams, and you will know that we are not alone in the universe – and that we never have been.

I have been shown that the universe is structured like a holographic onion. There are thousands of distinct layers, all interwoven, all interconnected, and all structured with living patterns of life forms connecting and sharing knowledge amongst each other. Within each and every layer there exists this multitude of life, from the absolute bizarre in appearance, to the breathtakingly beautiful and angelic.

Man through the ages, and a multitude of disciplines and techniques, has communicated with some of these uncharted worlds, from the Mystics and Shamans of old, to the Mediums and Remote Viewers of today.

The dialogues enclosed are a few of my communications with these lifeforms, sometimes creative, sometimes informative, but always a doorway to higher consciousness and understanding of the intricate nature of the universe we inhabit.

April, 2000

The location was at Brenda's, and the usual circle group were present. We all take our cardinal positions within the relative darkness of the small warm living room. The lights are all dimmed except the guiding light of the central candle. I closed my eyes, relaxed, and the journey began.

This conversation was with a life form with no discernable form, but the voice was male, deep, penetrating and resounding around me with a very reassuring and confident strength. For the purpose of identification we shall call him 'the voice'.

"Many races are working with you as you realise your place in the order of things. Bodies are changing and evolving to new heights, and with this comes discomfort and pain. Fortunately we are here to guide and help you, others in the past were not so lucky.

Mankind is on the precipice of involvement in a universal community, and his development over the next few years is key to this."

I asked "Where do we fit into this?"

"This information is given to you for a purpose, each of your minds will guide others near and far, helping to ease the pain of this evolutionary process. Nothing is clear, and pathways are not yet created, only envisaged. There are also others taking a close interest, others with not such a spiritual growth in mind, so we are carefully watching and waiting. As you probably know we do not rush, time does not exist for us, we are time. If we so desire we can stop the flow of time all around us, and wander in the amazing unfolding geometric patterns of life as they pass us by.

Many eons ago we started to work with you humans, helping the first man acknowledge himself and his separateness from the environment he was within. We are in the same process again now, only it is fraught with danger as not even we know the final end."

As I stopped to record this conversation in my notebook it became clear to me that this felt like a spiritual support group, I had a strong feeling of a structured environment created to help people like us – life forms - who are new and less understanding, adapt to the ways of the universe. They also gave the impression yet again that this was a global message, that it should all be recorded and if possible, one day shown to as many as possible.

I was next shown in images the acceleration of human consciousness and how recent advances in technology increase the speed of this process. One of the main concerns shown to me was that when humans eventually realise their potential, then some of us will use this knowledge in a negative way, and this will be on a universal scale. This will happen when we have learnt that there are no limitations to the human soul and the universe. I saw that this is one of their biggest concerns for the future of mankind, not in technology, global warming, pollution, or war, but in man's realisation that we are Gods, and by being gods how we then affect the whole universe.

A WARNING

Man is what he believes.
- Anton Chekhov (1860 - 1904)

June , 2000
Location - Brenda's house. The whole circle group was present. The voice returned.

"In the time before the darkness you will gather as a group, as a system in defiance of all that you believe. Each of you is a separate tool or element that is instrumental to the ongoing training, transmutation and transgression of will. There will be a time when you are tested, as others on another deeper, darker path watch closely your movements with envious eyes."

This channeled message sparked within me visions of a coming conflict, I could clearly see the representation of a battle, not a physical battle but a spiritual battle, a battle for the soul of man. This stage of our development with the higher life forms definitely had the feelings of training akin to spiritual sparring sessions.

Many of the meetings involved moving my consciousness from one point to another, experiencing the feeling as I moved through objects and walls feeling the levels of wood, stone, paint and fibre as I moved.

The meditations became more intense, and strange new concepts and ways of looking at the universe and experiences within this, were shown and explained to us. The life forms we communicated with always seemed to have a profound knowledge of future events, and at the same time the feelings we all picked up on were - that trouble lay ahead for us all.

KNOWLEDGE OF THE COMING.

The beginning of knowledge is the discovery of something we do not understand.
*- **Frank Herbert** (1920 - 1986)*

July, 2000
Location – Brenda's. All were present from the group.

After a very long intensive meditation to calm the body and mind, I ventured into the pulsating trunk of the central portal and was taken down and through one of the twisting branches to a location very deep within space. After an acclimatisation pause a conversation with the life form 'the voice' ensued.

"What do you have planned for the group?" I asked

"A quest for knowledge, for good, for power. Individually you will be put aside as duty calls you to arms in defiance. Strange, and wonderful times are near. The winds of time are changing and the balance is shifting in the favour of those who move against us.

Legions of trained and untrained marching forward under one banner, a banner of hidden darkness.

Each of you will learn and warn others of this impending time of conflict, teaching the open breasted spiritual pathways through the dark binding vines that will seek to crush and envelope you."

Shocked and astounded I asked "Who is the enemy?"

"The battle will be with people, ordinary people but with a will not of their own."

"But - why us?"

"You were chosen long ago, your skills individual but combined in circumstances. Power, imagination, hope and freedom. Nothing is left to chance, things are seen and sensed in the past and future that foretold the coming and the rising of man to his place in the cosmos."

"Will this be physical?"

"Yes and no, but what is physical? Where does your soul end and your body begin. There is no straightforward easy answer – there just is…."

"How long till this happens?" I enquired.

"Soon, preparation is the key. The others are being hunted too! Time is the key!"

"You mentioned others being prepared?"

"Yes, you are not alone, no one person or group holds the answers to it all – not even us! We are unable to predict the outcome, but are trying to help put a balance in the playing field."

"Who are you?"

"We are the wind in the trees, the slow breath of dying life, and the crying scream of a newborn. We are life and death, the universe and the individual. We are God."

"What God?" I asked.

"In every question there already resides the answer."

The life form then bade me farewell, as it was time for me to adjust my essence to the return cycle and slowly push the travelled parts of me back towards home. I say push because within these deeper meditative states I find it very hard to come back, the feeling of total expansion of consciousness leaves a deep feeling of loss at any thoughts of return to the body, so much so that the physical comeback process gets very intense. It is only the rhythmic spasms of the physical body, and the automatic patterns of breathing, that force this action. Breathing plays a major part in the process as it once again emerges from its slumber and rhythmically pulls you home with each deep, resounding breath.

On returning, I reflected on the session and felt a heavy, confused heart. The life form had parted knowledge of a massive importance. I was stunned and shocked, the relevance of information so profound if it were true, would affect all of mankind.

It was clear that humanity was heading for times of upheaval. It was also clear that this involved human kind joining a 'cosmic community'. Would this be an answer to the question of UFO's and alien abductions that have followed man through the last sixty years, or was man on the verge of discovering the answer to some exotic technology or spiritual insight? But above all who and what was this 'dark force' that seemed to be watching and stalking us – now these are questions I can only ponder.

THE DARK ONES CIRCLE

"When you start this journey of cosmic enlightenment, a child walks in to the forest, when he reach is the other side he walks out a God."
- ***Unknown life form*** - *August 13, 2000*

All four of the group were in attendance as usual. The warm down process seemed uneventful and we all progressed down the path of a deep meditative state. I moved into the swirling mass of the portal and was instantly transported deep into space and I stopped moving. I looked around and found myself floating, upright looking out over the vast horizon of space. Millions of stars flowed in the distance like shimmering sparkles on a river at night. Deep in the distance to my left was a tendril belt of luminescent blue cloud with three bright yellow stars glowing from within its folds.

The air shimmered in front of me like small heat waves radiating outwards and I instantly felt a second presence. It was the voice.

"We are all journeymen sipping from the ancient cup of knowledge. All seeking the key to enlightenment, but never fully achieving it. We play this endless game of cat and mouse with our immortal soul, learning but also teaching as we wander through the pathways of life."

I barely had the time to take these beautiful comments in, when I felt a second presence. The air around the circle group crackled and became incredibly dense. I could sense a thick heavy darkness take shape from the air around us and form itself into a loose indistinct shadow of a man. The shadow was tall, the precise borders of its shape hard to define as it was always in constant motion. The shadow moved fast, like a thick dense cloud of black smoke loosely formed into the shape of a hooded man. Purposely moving behind me it made me quickly turn in fear. I could feel the shadow as it swiftly circled around the group, its presence making the hair on the back of my neck crackle with electrical fear. It then started laughing with a gurgling, high-pitched tone cackling out loud whilst glancing in my direction. Faster and faster it sped around us, just outside of the protective reach of the circle. Round and round it went, at times too fast for my eyes to make out a clear shape to the form. Its voice now changing as it whispered our names with a deep menacing rasp one after another, over and over. I could sense the intimidating nature of this, it wanted us to know it knew who we were, it wanted us to be scared. Then as quickly as it had formed, it was gone. The thick dense form just seemed to evaporate in mid flight. The heaviness instantly cleared, and like the breaking of clouds on a sunny day I felt a warmth and light re-enter the room. The life form 'the voice' had also gone, at what point during the visitation I do not know. I awoke from the meditation faster than usual and with heaviness in my heart. I knew something bad was out there, it had a purpose which involved us, the group, me. And it knew our names.

I never discussed this and other shadow encounters with the rest of the group. I had an overwhelming feeling that it would do more harm than good to involve them. So I kept these intrusions to myself, and there were more of them to come.

AMETHYST GELS

Not only is the universe stranger than we imagine
it is stranger than we can imagine.
*- **Sir Arthur Eddington** (1882 - 1944)*

The cold wind of February rolled in and 'The Group' was starting to experience some interesting explorations once again. As usual we met at Brenda's; we took our places at the cardinal compass points and one by one slipped in to the deep folds of advanced meditation.

Following the usual pattern, I travelled deep, past the stages of separation, into the void, and deeper past this into the darkness, with only the deep rhythmical sound of my breathing as company and as my anchor to the physical world. I could feel my mind float free of the physical constraints, the body was felt no more and the mind expanded in all directions filling the space around me. I could feel movement as I spiralled through a thick black void, tumbling through space for what seemed like an age.

Upon reaching my destination, almost like floating, I slowly touch down on a surface, but with no force of gravity. I have a body but it's not physical, it's like a jelly fish see through and iridescent as the energy flows from the Chakra points to the extremities like pin pricks of light travelling along glowing veins. I look up and as I do the environment around me takes form before my eyes as it manifests out of the darkness.

Directly in front of me are a group of very tall darkly robed figures. The robes flow from their slender forms and drape across the floor surface and overlap in a sea of dark. With a gesture and a nod from one of the beings, I found myself instantly transported to a new location. On hastily looking around my new environment it was spherical shaped. The walls seemed to be constructed of a material not unlike the look of an amethyst crystal, with deep purples overlapping with shards of sparkled light. I was immersed in a thick purple, living gel. This gel rippled with energy and moved like a heavy viscous liquid. My movement was limited, but without panicking, I found myself wading slowly in and through this strange gel-like experience. Like so many of the experiences in meditative states, before I had time to completely examine the experience I was pulled backward out from the sphere with a heavy, fast expulsion. I could almost hear the sucking noise as my body separated from the viscous amethyst jelly.

Once out of the sphere I was once again in front of the tall-cloaked beings who looked at me with an expectant, pregnant period of time. On reflection I feel the gel was some kind of cleaning or acclimatisation process, maybe we as humans carry infectious elements even in a non-physical realm. Fully sterilised I now stood before the cloaked beings.

For some reason something told me it was time for me to do something, that it was for me they were waiting for. With this I held out my left hand palm up and looked at my palm with a deep concentration. From out of thin air above my palm, circular shapes started to grow and form. These were pink, red and white, and as I looked on with astonishment, the shapes formed a cube and the coloured molecule-like spheres of light rotated in and out. This process lasted a few seconds then one by one the molecules peeled off, rising up and to the left and dissipated in to the air. This demonstration, or light show, seemed to have achieved the desired effect, and with a gentle nod from the lead being I was catapulted backward with an intense pull from the rear of my solar plexus. The space behind me opened and warped in a circular motion. The journey home had started.

As I fell back towards the state of emergence from the meditation a voice from all around me said "the time of adjustment is nearly over."

Five minutes later, as I approached the final stages of warm-down, and was near to physical reality, questions raced through my mind. "Was that it?" the sum total of this universal knowledge was "it's nearly over" no "sorry to bother you", no "sorry we're about to do this" – or no – "do you mind?"

As I re-adjusted to my being in a physical state I gently simmered as these thoughts raced through my mind. You will probably go there too! It is sometimes hard to accept that parts of our growth and exploration of other realms is based around the help and knowledge of other beings. Who, it has to be said, talk in riddles, in simple truth, and very, very bluntly.

On later reflection, I feel an important stage had been passed that day. I sensed a great respect and feeling of pride from the beings, at what I had created. I now understand it was the creation of the spherical lightshow that I had created, that had impressed and sealed my journey home. The lesson was that in their world, the nonphysical world, I could create anything I needed from myself and everything around me. Everything was already there - the intent, me-the catalyst, the energy flowing in and through everything. Now when I look back I feel that this was a defining moment. A time where I learnt a skill that one-day would save me from great harm.

CHANGES

The universe is change; our life is what our thoughts make it.
-Marcus Aurelius Antoninus (121 AD - 180 AD)

During the next six months, the interaction with dimensional life forms centered on developing and changing parts of my physical and non-physical bodies. These we were told, were always needed for our bodies to adapt to the different conditions and developments that were to come.

The first series of changes are achieved by taking you into very deep meditative states. The process takes about twenty plus minutes in real time, but in meditation time it only feels like a minute. These states are so deep that no physical sensation can be felt from the physical body. It's as if the physical doesn't exist, and the whole of you is floating in an empty void. We call this process 'Total separation'. For a short period of time you can dwell and experience this new sensation before a new series of sensations start. The physical body starts to vibrate at a rate that feels very high, and at the same time strange and slightly nauseating. The heart speeds up, so does your breathing rhythm and the conscious mind starts to ask panicky questions like "what's happening to me?" And "Is this right?" This forces the body to produce adrenalin, which in turn amplifies the whole sensation leaving two clear options, allow the fear to root and abort the session, or face the fear and ride the sensations through. The first few times into this uncharted territory I aborted. I achieved abortion by using every ounce of power and effort I could muster and forced myself out of the deep state without any slow warm-down period. This alone is very hard and can leave the body in a state of temporary shock at the instant transition. During my first experience in this stage of development, the whole process of sensations caught me so unawares I felt as though I was having a heart attack as the vibrational intensity increased, and spread through me from the center of the solar plexus outwards to my finger tips. The fear of this was the factor that led me to abort, as a great writer once said 'fear is the mind killer'. If you, on your journeys of exploration, encounter this developmental stage, then do not panic, try to work with the sensations. If the fear is too much - abort, there is always the next time. When the time is right, feel the vibrations ripple through you, work with them as they move, and in time they will fade as you become one with them, and before you know it the process is over and the wave is behind you.

CHANGES

The rapid vibration change is extreme but also a needed passage. During my experiences through this stage I found that on encountering the fear and not allowing it to push me from the sensations, that they were very enjoyable. I liken them to a feeling of fluttering from the inside outwards, mixed with a rush of excitement and a glowing feeling. On passing this stage and dwelling on the experiences, I could also feel a slight movement and sensation of manipulation. These were around both my eyes and throat. On asking what was happening, I was informed that this was a process of adaptation and changing parts of my being on a dimensional level and not the physical, and not to worry. I could not see who or what was touching or prodding me, but only felt the slight brush like gentle movements in a caressing way as they worked.

I have experienced similar sensations through my years of psychic development, but generally not after such an intense experience. Every person on a pathway of exploration will feel these changes at key times. Again, don't be afraid, work with them, change is necessary for you to advance.

These changes usually are centered on the mystical places of the body's seven main Chakra points. Moving down through the body these are the Crown, Third eye, Throat, Heart, Solar plexus, Groin and the base or Root

Chakra. These ancient points of energy form a solid rod of communication and sensory traffic throughout the entire body. At key points in a spiritual development cycle, life forms will interact and calibrate your charka system as you progress. These become mystical doorways, which open up new worlds and possibilities. So when you feel that slight helping hand like a breeze across one of these seven key points, then say a gentle thank you to the helpers, and remember new journeys await you.

The word Chakra means 'wheel' in Sanskrit. 'Wheel' because each Chakra when viewed can be seen spinning with the energy flow that it creates. Chakra points are key to spiritual development and with time and effort you can envision not only your own but those of others as well. I see the Chakra points as closed buds of lotus flowers when not in use. Closed to the everyday world, allowing everyday existence to go on. Upon opening for spiritual or psychic work I see them unfold like the petals of a flower in the rays of the sun. They open and spread their petals wide revealing radiant colours and energy outwards and through the body and soul.

THE BASE CHAKRA

The first of the seven major centres is located at the coccyx at the base of the spine and it is usually called the root or base chakra. Its associated element is earth and it corresponds to the sense of smell, physical energy and vitality. This is the centre we can turn to if we need physical strength. The colour for this Chakra is red.

THE SACRAL CHAKRA

The second Chakra point is found just below the navel and is called the Sacral Centre. It is linked with the adrenals and the release of adrenaline into the body. Its element is water and if this centre is out of balance your 'flight or fight' response may be over active. This centre also has a cleansing function by filtering out negative influences. The colour for this Chakra point is orange.

THE SOLAR PLEXUS

The next centre is found just below the breastbone and is Solar Plexus Chakra. It is linked to the digestive system, stomach, pancreas, and liver. Its associated element is fire. This Chakra is the storehouse for our positive energy. Also it is the link between the mind and the emotions. An imbalance here can lead to 'butterflies' and digestive disorders. The colour of the Solar Plexus Chakra is yellow.

THE HEART CHAKRA

In the centre of the chest is the heart centre. This controls the immune system. It is the 'heart' of emotions such as love, tenderness, compassion and honesty. The energies from this centre affect the heart, lungs, upper chest, and back. Its element is air and its Chakra colour is green.

THE THROAT CHAKRA

The next Chakra is found at the top of the throat. Its element is Ether and it's linked with communication and self-expression through thoughts, writing and speech. It is linked to the thyroid gland, which controls metabolic rate. It also influences the throat, ears, nose, mouth and neck. This Chakra is Blue.

THE THIRD EYE CHAKRA

This journey now brings us to the sixth Chakra which lies in the centre of the forehead. This is often given the name of 'the third eye'. It is found above and between the eyebrows and is linked to the pituitary and pineal glands. This Chakra is the seat of higher consciousness and spiritual powers. Psychic, clairvoyance telepathy and other related skills are generated by this Chakra, and it also controls the body's eyes, nerves, head and brain. The Chakra colour is a deep indigo.

THE CROWN CHAKRA

Normally known as the 'crown centre' this is also known as the seat of the soul. As with the third eye centre this centre is also linked to the pituitary and pineal glands. It is associated with the perfection of mind, body and spirit. Its Chakra colour is violet but in reality this Chakra is a mass of shimmering lights and energy from the whole visual spectrum and beyond.

THE HUMAN CHAKRA SYSTEM

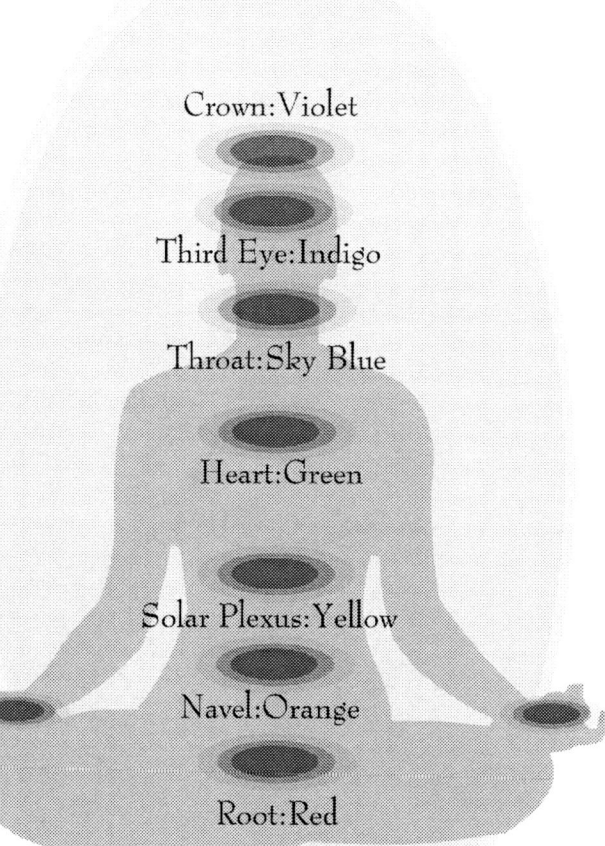

A WATCHER

Reality is that which, when you stop believing in it it doesn't go away.
- Philip K. Dick (1928 - 1982)

During the first group meeting of the New Year, I was to accidentally meet one of the most interesting life forms talked about in esoteric books and mythological stories including the bible, The Watchers.

The meditation went well. Despite my new anticipation at getting back into our travels after a long Christmas break, I slipped into the deeper states of consciousness like I had never been away. At the point of total separation when a part of you realises that all physical sensations are gone. A cold, sobering, awakening takes form. It feels akin to the waking sensation in a lucid dream. The point where the dreamer becomes aware he is dreaming. This point, this stage of realisation allows me to take a different part in the unfolding events. Early stages of meditative states only allow passenger experiences. These are like being a passenger in a car, watching the landscape and events unfold in front of you, but when something interesting is seen, you want the power to stop and to absorb the experience. The deeper stages are completely different. The physical detachment brings forth this realisation of control. The passenger state has faded, and for the first time total control of movement and experience is yours. This for me always happens in a deep place which is black, almost sterile, no sound, no feeling just a deep black void. On this occasion after the first few seconds of exhilarating realisation about my new freedom of movement, I noticed golden stars form from the void in front of me. Distance is impossible to tell in the void, but above me and not far away, sparkles of golden light fall from the darkness like bonfire night sparklers waving in the dark. The sparkles glitter as they fall slowly towards me falling on my head and shoulders, but with no physical feeling.

A movement from the left almost behind me spins me round and I face a life form. I almost jump in surprise as I find a grey cloaked being only feet away from me. As I study it closely, I can see a heavy, thick grey cloak reaching to a deep hooded opening where the face should be. I stare and try to find a detail, any detail from within the dark space, but find nothing. It feels like an age has passed, nothing is said, no movements made as I study this being, watching its every movement.

Eventually after my senses told me I was in no great danger I asked the life form a question "what are you?"

A soft voice neither male nor female replied "I am a Watcher."

Stupidly I asked "what are you doing?"

"Watching" came the reply.

"Watching what?" I enquired.

"Everything"

With this last comment, the life form turned and walked away into the darkness of the void that surrounded us. The whole overriding sensation from the watcher was of subtle neutrality. I sensed a feeling of impartiality in everything it was doing, and that what he was doing was of no importance to me. I sometimes think that maybe if I had not seen that movement, that the watcher would have done just that – watched And I would have been none the wiser.

A PSYCHIC WARRIOR

Wisdom is not finally tested in the schools, Wisdom cannot be passed from one having it to another not having it, Wisdom is of the soul, is not susceptible of proof, is its own proof.
*- **Walt Whitman** (1819 - 1892)*

We started the session like any other, all of us finding our own pace, slowing the physical functions of the body and allowing the mind to fill into the space within us. Within a short while I felt myself drop deeply as if a step had been taken off a cliff into a deep abyss.

After an age of falling I landed on a hard surface in a place of total darkness - a thick darkness hard to achieve in the real world, tainted by ambient vibrations and light. Slowly out of the dark in front of me light illuminated a shape about twenty feet away. Curiosity pulling at me I moved closer and in the dim light could make out the form of a large wolf. It was huge, muscular in the torso and stared with sparkling eyes, watching and glaring as if looking deep into my soul. I also sensed something new, something building and something felt wrong!

All around me from every angle, but at a distance, moving closer I could feel a dark presence. This drew closer and the consistency of it became clearer. It was oily but without oil or a wetness, and moved like smoke but it had a real dark and solid substance, and when it breathed, in and out with its long rasping noises, the hair on my neck tingled and stood upright as fear took hold.

The dark form had spread all around me and I felt trapped as it kept expanding and circled around and around, with its menacing whispering tentacles of dreadful noise. The wolf just sat there staring at me almost oblivious to the foreboding dark form. I didn't see it at first, but after a while it dawned on me, this wasn't a natural response from a wolf or any living form, if I could feel the crushing sense of dark evil that encircled us then a true creature definitely would. This wolf creature needed to be tested.

I had never used this technique before, but I had been taught it by my psychic mother, Brenda and many other teachers in many books throughout the years. Testing a life form in an altered state of consciousness is a standard technique – I had never used it because I felt I could always sense the intention of the life form, and could prepare a counter attack long before any dark attack would come. But now it was needed.

I focused all my attention on a space a few feet in front of me, and by simply asking and by focusing my thoughts; I created a bright intense ring of roaring fire. Then in the time old way, practiced by many people many times before me, I asked the wolf to declare its intentions and if he were a friend or foe the fire would tell. The wolf sat there watching, staring and not moving. Then suddenly, with a pounce it leapt at the fiery ring.

With an explosion, light radiated outward from the ring of fire. Large white ripples of light in bands radiated outward like those in a lake when a pebble is cast. There was no real sound but a vibration that shook my form and the waves spread past me and crashed into the evil life form that circled me a few feet away.

I could feel the heaving recoil of the dark form as the rings of light ripped through its dark tendrils smashing it into thousands of small pieces. These pieces seemed to float for a second like particles floating in space, and then as if acknowledged by defeat they dissipated and were gone.

I had been so preoccupied with the spectacle of the dark form that I had almost forgotten about the wolf, and turned around towards the fiery ring. Before me arranged in a neat circle patiently sat six wolves! Each of them watching me with those deep piercing eyes following my gaze and my every move. If a wolf could smile I swear these would have, as they sat there and watched with a silent smirk. Slowly my natural senses kicked in and I felt that these were friendly and that they wanted me to sit at the centre of their circle. Slowly and gingerly I crossed the darkness watching the faces of these beautiful creatures before me, I entered their circle and obediently following some instinctive but invisible lead, sat cross-legged in front of my new hosts.

Time passed, slowly at first but building rapidly over the minutes as they floated by into space. I could feel the swelling sensation of subtle energies as they built up and flowed all around us. Their energy grew, and as it grew so did an accompanying sound that seemed to vibrate through every area of my form. A single note not too dissimilar to the sound of meditating monks. Then without warning and in unison the wolves craned their necks skyward and thick white energy leapt from their eyes and mouths like beams of intense white light penetrating the darkness above us.

I looked up following the light and reaching far up into the dark void above me, the tendrils of light entwined and corkscrewed upwards like a mythical living beast. The tendrils reached up higher and higher and then stopped. They faltered motionless for a brief second then turned and fell, hurtling rapidly downwards – towards me! The last thing I remember is a large intense white flash that filled the whole of my vision.

The white faded and the edges of darkness started to filter back into the corners of my eyes, shaking my head as if to clear it from the brightness, I looked around. Sat head cocked to one side, its tongue dangling with a wet glistening edge was the single wolf. Its grey patchy fur now clearly visible with long thick hair slightly raised and rippled over the bones of its back. Without time to take it all in and think about the traumatising light, there came a voice. I knew instantly that it resonated from the wolf, still watching me patiently. "Welcome back – warrior." With this the wolf turned and trotted off into the darkness in front of me. A few seconds later it was gone, swallowed up by the blackness.

I sat there exhausted, confused and overwhelmed. The experiences crowded and jostled inside my mind fighting for a position of understanding – but it wasn't to come right now, as I recognised the familiar sensations of the portal opening behind me and the energies spinning and growing – It was time to go home.

Later that evening I wrote in detail all that happened. I could now see that as well as a test I was also given something. The energy that hit me like a bolt of lightening had empowered me with something. I felt different, something had changed. The wolf, life form whatever it was, was right, I felt it growing within me. I now had a new status, a new role, a warrior's path – a pathway within our hyperspace travels.

RIPPLES, WAVES AND SECRETS

If you reveal your secrets to the wind you should not blame the wind for revealing them to the trees.
- Kahlil Gibran (1883 - 1931)

The group started, I closed my eyes and instantly felt my tense worked muscles give in to the moment and start to relax as I molded into the couch. The portal arose as usual as a great spiraling mass of living energy that snaked about in the middle of our protective circle of light. Quicker than usual, I found myself travelling up and through one of the spiral's convoluted branches up and out into space.

Touchdown was a dark space, cold with hardly any stars in the distant horizon. Empty space swallowed me as I looked around for a point of reference. Instantly I felt the presence of a nearby life form, yet nothing was visible. If this were anywhere other than hyperspace then alarm bells would ring, sending adrenalin racing around the body, starting the natural defense mechanisms. In this case, although there was no physical form, the deep penetrating resonance of the life form penetrated the space all around me, and far off into the distance where it eventually dissipated – like mist. It was as if the life form was an extension of space itself.

My mind raced with confused impressions as I reached for a question to ask. But this wasn't needed as before me a vision started to unfold. Looking into the space in front of me, some of the stars started to move out of position. First one, then two more joined them, then others moving with a purpose like fairy lights dancing in the heavens. It soon became apparent that the star lights were moving into a structured formation. After these first ones took a position, many more quickly rushed forward as if to join the show - as if alive. Within moments star lights filled my vision in a huge arcing vision of sparkling life, and with a soundless thunderclap they filled the space between themselves and a large living screen of light appeared before me, suspended against the deep dark black of space.

From all around me a voice resounded with a clear, slightly feminine clarity. "Watch and you will see." I turned my head back and forth looking around trying to pinpoint the origin of the voice, but then focused on what was in front of me. The lights had formed a living rippling shape like a huge glowing cinema screen suspended in the darkness of space. As I watched, the bright white shape slipped into dull colours and surreal movie like imagery appeared all around me like a virtual IMax cinema experience with sitting room for one.

Images moved at great speed in and out of my vision, some were too fast to comprehend, huge vibrant images of crashing waves on a shore mixed with scenes of a star exploding and invisible waves radiating from its core millions of miles into space. The images were interspersed and overlapped with words, sentences and symbols, but the speed was just too fast to take it all in. It seemed to last forever, like a pop video on fast forward. A huge amount of visual information raced in and out of my subconscious which was becoming numb with all the visual stimuli.

Then it stopped suddenly. The imagery was gone, and the ghost like trail of the last images started to fade from my vision, and so too was the living screen. There was nothing, but the view over the horizon into the infinite expanse of space and beyond and the quiet vacuum that the experience left like an awkward pregnant pause.

"Close your eyes" whispered the soft voice out of nowhere. I closed my eyes feeling the darkness slip around me like a comforting cloak.

I waited, and slowly from my darkness a speck of light grew as it hurtled out of the void bringing the imagery shown to me on the screen in slower chunks. This time I relaxed, watched and learnt.

When it finished, I slowly opened my eyes almost expecting to see something as they opened, squinting to adjust to the real darkness of space. "You see" said the voice "waves - the underlying structure of the universe."

I did see, not clearly there was too much information for that, but I did get the gist of it all. They were showing me a constant, an underlying principle they said was a common property for the smallest of things to the largest, from the quantum to the universal. 'Waves.' Light, energy, darkness, and life itself, all travelling in waves of different shapes and sizes all interwoven in a large tapestry of conflicting, bouncing ripples.

These waves ripple throughout the universe transferring information about everything within the trillions of bouncing ripples. I was shown waves of energy travelling at speeds faster than the speed of light, passing galaxies, planets and bright stars burning like our sun. Next the vision changed and violet rings of energy radiated out from a central point of white light. As my view followed the bands as they expanded outward colliding and mixing with others. The colours mixed as a violet band hit a faint yellow wave and tendrils of violet permeated the yellow band like an expanding stream. Following the bands as they expanded further, I looked back to the central white point and was astonished to see that this had transformed into the thunderous beating heart inside the body of a curled up embryo. I bet that in this moment I looked really funny. Suspended in the darkness of space, God knows where, with a huge grin and my mouth held wide open as I for a moment try to grasp the enormity of what was communicated.

In front of me I could sense the pleasure the life form gained from me and the experience it had given. The space around me buzzed with a feeling of accomplishment, energy and pride. Like the pride I get as a parent as I watch my son accomplish something wondrous and new. The manifestation of this 'parent's smile' now radiated through the space all around me, enveloping me in a warm radiant glow of universal love.

Behind me I sensed the vibrations of the approaching portal home and the long journey back into my body. I said thank you to the life form and felt the acknowledgement ripple back through the space like a confirming nod of the head. I was on my way back home again.

I feel that I gained something that day. I look back now and try, and try to visualize all the imagery that raced through me. But to no avail, some of it has gone. I sometimes feel a little inadequate at not entirely being able to understand the whole message. And maybe someone else could have remembered and understood more. But all this is not to be, I was shown the vision and told to spread the messages – so this is what I'm doing.

The next time you look out of the window and see the top of a tree moving back and forth in the throws of the wind, remember that everything is connected. You, me, the trees, the stars, planets and the very space itself in between all of this. There is no separation, only the illusion of it. Man on his journey asking his eternal questions like the meaning of life, already has the answers at his very fingertips. In its most simplistic form – and it is all down to waves.

THINGS TO COME – CONFLICT AND HOPE!

The real distinction is between those who adapt their purposes to reality and those who seek to mold reality in the light of their purposes.
- ***Henry Kissinger** (1923 -)*

This entire section 'things to come' has been split into three chapters. These prophetic journeys into hyperspace detail a future conflict, hidden adversaries, and balance. All three chapters come together to form a picture of events unfolding around us, by whom and why they involve man.

As usual we met in the familiar setting of Brenda's comfy living room. After our initial good-natured greetings we all quickly slid into our individual altered states of consciousness, we settled in our chairs and began our travels deep into hyperspace.

Unlike the usual dreamlike descent my vision exploded with vast scenes of carnage and mayhem. All around me I saw fast, blurred images of death and chaos, a montage of destruction. This shocked me, but as with all psychic explorations you can't choose the ride, so I had to sit there as the images pass through me. The feeling is of total bedlam, a time in the future, a great conflict with massive loss of life. Surrounding this whole vision was the strong heavy sense of a battle between good and evil, not just good and bad men and their reasons, but a larger sense of evil, pure and intense. The images raced faster and I could see the faces of children sitting down at their school desks, they hear a noise rolling and getting louder as it rushes towards them. Then they are gone - swallowed in a rolling wave of destruction. I see the wide-eyed terror on their faces as they panic and rush towards the exit, but it's too late. I then see them crushed in the ruins of the school.

Before the impact of the first images fade they are replaced with overhead views of marching soldiers. Lots of them, side by side in rows all clean and fresh uniformed and presented in long marching lines snaking along and out of sight into the distance. The images blur again and scenes of an immense battle replaced the calm. Great clouds of dust carried and stretched by the wind fall on fields ripped apart by the carnage of war. Dust falls on men lying, open and gaping, their limbs stretched and bent into positions unnatural for the human form. The dust falls on tangled blackened rags of metal.

Things to Come – Conflict and Hope!

Dust falls on carcasses of misshapen buildings, grotesquely deformed in the haze of the vision.

With all the effort I have left inside of me, I wrench myself from the carnage and out of the deep meditation, bringing me back to the physical world with a jolt. At first I find it hard to catch my breath. I look around with physical eyes not fully understanding where I was, or how I had moved from the encompassing vision of pain to a small dark room, full of total peace. Then slowly, like blood draining back into a dead limb, my physical senses return and I breathe a deep sigh of relief as I fade back into the physical world.

I spend the next ten minutes recording my observations like I had been taught. All the while questions are racing through me about what I had just experienced and what they all meant. The death, destruction, and the evil sense of waste that permeated the experience. I can't explain it but I knew this was in the future. An immense conflict involving all nations, and ultimately leading to massive destruction and a massive loss of life. Like the biblical battle of Armageddon, the ultimate and final battle between what's left of the good in the world and the evil that walks in the background.

Determined not to let the rest of the meditation time go to waste, I relaxed my mind and took a deep breath. This helped in releasing all the previous imagery, and once again I slipped into a deep meditation where I entered the portal and off I went, out into the void.

The stars stretched into long wavy iridescent wriggling lines behind me into the deep blue hazy darkness. Within minutes I was there. I landed with a thump that echoed around me. This sound told me that the surface was solid and it felt artificial. I looked around and saw a large open square courtyard. The floor is decoratively patterned in hues of browns that form large geometric shapes that unfold all around me. In different areas of the courtyard, huddled in small groups of two and three are small people clothed in white flowing cloth. I concentrate, trying to form a clear picture of the nearest life form and as the picture clarifies before me, I stand and gasp on seeing something unlike I have ever seen before. Starting from the top they have a large bulbous head. Not like a human form where the head is round, but these are large and have a regular almost square look. The head is a tanned brown in colour, not unlike tanned leather. The top of the head is shrouded with folds where the brow would be, three or four of theses that cascade over the top of the head like undulating waves. Wispy, long, but sparsely arranged hair can be seen as it catches the light on the top parts of the head as it disappears over the back. On what would be the face sits a single large central eye. The iris is black and looks incredibly large as I see it expand whilst searching for me. At both the edges of the eye it looks as though it has two areas that look like a human tear glands, which reach both over and under the eye framing it with more lines of the same tanned skin. There is no mouth, no nose and no ears. In fact the head seems to just mould into the rest of the body and I find it strange that there is no neck. From the head it just moves down following the shape from the head. As my eye moves downwards I notice that the garment is folded with a collar like grove that encircles the form indicating where the head ends and the body begins, or so it seems to me a human. The garment itself shines when caught by the light, but also moves and looks like a heavy material. The garment has sleeves created by folds and in these, I can see what appears to be a hand. Like the head the digits look squared off and instead of five this form has three digits or fingers. These are arranged in a triangular shape and I get the feeling that they have a joint that allows them to bend inwards like the arms of a crane but I do not see this, I just feel it.

The creature I am studying moves towards me. I don't see it move the long folds of the robe covering any feet or leg-like appendages. In fact it gave the impression of floating as the form moved across the patterned floor squares towards me. The nearer it got the more I thought – this can't be real. The creature stopped in front of me about six feet away. I felt that it didn't really want the job of communicating but it may have been invoked by my choosing of him when I first scanned the room.

I could sense the moments slide between us, an uncomfortable silence as we both stood there and stared at each other, evaluating. For all I know he may have found me as strange as I found him. I knew we had to communicate, so to break the stillness I said "I need to test you – I need to know your intent." The creature answered with a gentle nod. With this I felt a tug from behind, and a hyperspace movement vibrated and sucked us through as the background and the creature blurred in my vision and we tumbled through space.

Suddenly, and without any warning, the movements and blurring stopped. My hazy vision also took a few seconds to also stop moving and as it does I see the creature is still with me and that he must have travelled too. I quickly look around, the surroundings are different. It's still artificial with stone patterned flooring, but now a different pattern, and a different set of brown hues and shades. In the far distance I can make out walls that stretch up high above me, so high that I cannot see the top and it becomes blurred by distance. Other life forms flow across the floor in the distance in the same manner generating an etheric feeling of gliding over the surface, almost elegant.

I gather my thoughts and strong impressions permeate me with the overwhelming feeling that I'm in a vast library. But I don't see any books. "I can see you have a library" I said to the creature.

"This is one of the reasons why you are here", was the response, not in an audible voice but in a voice that filled my mind and that flowed from everywhere around me. It's a strange sensation hearing the voice of another but with no movement of lips or a mouth to confirm the sound – it's strange and even now it's hard to establish the placement of the voice other than by the actual feeling of the sound.

The creature held out his hand, and for the first time I could clearly see the stumpy looking wrinkled three digits on it. Above it, blue sparkles of light appeared from thin air and swirled in a circular movement. As these speed up the light grows in intensity, then from nowhere the lights form into a single orb of blue light that hovers above the creature's outstretched hand.

"It's a record it's our knowledge, our history and more importantly our mistakes." Said the creature. "We need you to take charge of it for us." At this I backed away saying hurried excuses like "you've got to be joking – I'm definitely the wrong person, this is way too heavy." The creature looked at me confused, as if trying to understand my response. After a long second of thought and when he saw I had eventually run out of excuses it said "You're not alone – others have been trusted with the information. One day you will find them, this will be important for you."

Now please let's digress here a while, until you've been travelling psychically it's very hard to say no to these life forms. For a start you're God knows where, with God knows what, and they always seem to have a lot to say but never say it straight. The closest thing on earth I can think of are very wise men who answer your questions but in a manner that makes you work for the answer. Times that feeling by one hundred, and you start to understand the presence that these forms radiate. Sometimes I feel that NO is just not an option and that it has already been decided that I would say YES, I just haven't physically said it yet.

So reluctantly I agreed. But only if the creature allowed me to experience life from its point of view, I wanted to step inside this great bulbous creature and see what he saw, and to feel the world how he felt it. I watched as the creature seemed to think on this. The big furrowed brow above his one eye creasing as my comments gestated. With a nod – it was agreed, I was to merge with this creature. For a moment I panicked, what was I doing? Why had I asked for this? Was I crazy? Hurried thoughts of flight ran through me and were quickly swept away by a calming inner voice that replaced them. It was to be. Resigned to this fate I could feel my body already on its path of relaxation as my aura expanded and glowed as we moved together.

My eyes were closed but my senses told me the moment our two energy fields touched. From the dark spaces behind my eyes, tendrils of blue light flickered across my darkness as I felt my form or shape push and pull into a new form, a new space. The creature was heavy. I could feel its dense form all around me almost restricting. I sensed that physical movement was possible but not as important to them as to us. I started to understand that their limbs and organs were in an age old process of evolution which regressed them. With the need for their use growing less they were discarded over the eons and replaced with other faculties and limbs. This was why only one eye and the most rudimentary of arms and fingers. The vision through the remaining eye though was awesome. I saw the surrounding surfaces and creatures glowing with a rippled moving light. They had form, but the light told a picture of the creature. Like a psychic summary. I could tell at a glance what the creature was doing, its state of mind and its purpose. Not in-depth but instantly the knowledge was available. I don't even know how it was perceivable – I just knew. The actual vision was wider than ours, and fast movement had a strange distorted effect on the radiating energy causing it to blur. For a brief moment I was allowed to feel the extent of the creature's mind, and it was vast. This only lasted a fraction of a second, but it must be like how a blind man feels when he can see for the first time. The world suddenly gets bigger. The closest I can describe to this feeling is spending time in a small cramped space then moving to a large empty echoing room. This instantaneous feeling of massive expansiveness is the feeling I briefly experienced. After this moment closed I had an incredible instant yearning for more. A hunger for the expansiveness ripped through me like an intolerable thirst. With this I felt the creature start to pull away and the thirst grew as I was pulled back into my own smaller form.

I felt like a hungry child yearning for more food as it's wrenched away from its mother's nipple, and boy did I fell like screaming. After the forced separation I could feel an uneasiness emanate from the creature. I knew it had accidentally allowed me to see too much and was worried about the effects this may have. As I was being dragged back to my own form I felt small, so very small. I felt so inadequate and I was truly humbled. I sensed that these creatures had been working alongside mankind for millennia. Every contact was part of a larger plan with a grand scale. All contact is non-physical and many of us have been contacted. The reason for this – I don't really know, it wasn't given to me. I also felt a sense of sadness from the creatures. Not heavy, but a little sadness and maybe this was towards us as human beings. I felt their sadness for what we are, and what we could be, if only we knew how.

The creature backed away from me and once again held out its hand. Just like before the air sparkled like magic and from nothing formed the intense blue ball of radiant light. The light moved, it rose up from his hand with a soft controlled graceful movement. Within seconds it had reached the mid way point between us and was level with my eye line. I knew it was now time for my part of the bargain, I closed my eyes. With a soft sigh I let all the air leave my lungs, and as I did this the light entered me through my brow into the invisible third eye.

Everything went white. After a while the bright white energy dimmed from my view and was slowly replaced with the familiar darkness of my closed eyes. I opened them. The creature was gone. In fact they were all gone. I felt alone and naked. This vulnerability didn't last long, as from behind my right shoulder I could feel and see the edges of my vision stretch and elongate as the space behind me stretched back towards my physical dimension, and the long journey back across time and space to physical reality began.

THINGS TO COME – DARK REVELATIONS

Victorious warriors win first and then go to war, while defeated warriors go to war first and then seek to win.
- ***Sun-tzu*** *(~400 BC), The Art of War.*

They came out of the darkness of hyperspace like a bullet. One minute I was speeding headlong through my created portal out into hyperspace enjoying the colours and spectacles of space as it spiralled by, the next I see three distended dark forms streak past at high speed, travelling faster than myself. Shock ripped through my body and it took all my training to stop myself from shaking free of the meditative state and running as far away as I could from these dark creatures.

After a few seconds the initial shock subsided, but on looking out into the spiralling stars, colours and hyperspace, the forms were still there, keeping pace just in front of me. The lead form then seemed to look backwards straight into my eyes – and I swear I could see him laughing; only it had no face, just a dark empty hole where one should be.

So this was it! Here I was alone, speeding through a network of multi dimensions with three menacing looking creatures that looked as though they were about to give me the equivalent of a psychic mugging, and all I could do was sit back and enjoy the ride.

I landed with a thump. No gentle touchdown like usual, but a crunch as I landed with one knee embedded in some kind of hard baked and cracked surface. As I looked around it appeared desolate, with a cracked jigsaw looking texture to the surface like it had once rained long ago, but since then the sun had baked the earth until it had distorted and broken into submission. Far away on the horizon I could see iridescent clouds stream past craggy, fierce looking dark cliffs. The sky itself was a mixture of purple hues and angry rolling cloud formations. Weirdly, it was bleak but kind of beautiful at the same time.

With the strange environment I had all but forgotten the journey and the unexpected travel companions, but this didn't last long as out of the rolling clouds, three dark shapes broke away and at speed came at me from the distant horizon.

I stood there alone, lost somewhere in hyperspace. I glanced around looking for cover, looking for anything, but there was nothing, nothing to hide behind – or was there? Inspiration from out of the blue took over me like some kind of instinctive reflex action. I dropped to one knee, feeling the ground crack and give way beneath me. I felt myself look down towards the earth, I then closed my eyes and concentrated hard.

Out of my psychic vision I could feel the three forms hurtle through the air towards me. Their presence revealed by a sensation of dark dread that moved before them like a wave of despair. Closer, they were getting closer now, I could feel them. Whatever my instincts had forced me to do; it didn't feel like it was working.

Then they were upon me. They descended from above like some dark bird of prey, talons outstretched and I was the prey! I was still flinching downward in defence of the impending attack, when the creatures stopped with a crash. They had hit some kind of shield that seemed to surround me. As they shuddered against this invisible protection, ripples of contacted purple energy radiated away from the impact point revealing the guard that covered my kneeling position like a trapped bubble under water.

This didn't stop the creatures, it just seemed to anger them and I could hear the screech as they repeatedly rammed the protective barrier again and again.

Their actions seemed to go on forever, although it was probably only a minute in reality. After a while, their attempts at getting me slowly calmed down, until there was nothing! I looked up, lifting my head from the protection of my curled up form. They weren't gone, they were floating a few yards away just in front of where I lay curled. I felt confident enough to look longer at my adversaries, and through the last dissipating arcs of purple energy, I saw their forms. One was taller than the others, not by much but enough to be noticeable; this one was positioned in the centre protectively flanked by the two slightly smaller dark forms. They took the shape of humans, but loosely wrapped in pitch black draped shrouds, that trailed behind in long streams of flapping moving darkness that seemed to accentuate their movements. I eyed them closely and could see them move in a bobbing motion with the flow of the wind. Each felt different with a different personality, but with no really apparent discernable features or difference that I could physically see, I just felt the differences. The form on my right was a female, I don't know how I knew this but having this knowledge didn't make my situation any better!

I needed to move, so I stretched out an arm. I saw it touch and expand the barrier as I extended – "good" I thought, it moves with me. I wouldn't have to stay curled up in a hunched ball in the dirt, and with this I tentatively rose to my feet, whilst all the time staring straight ahead expecting another attack. The attack didn't come, and as I rose from my protection the shield around me also rose and the dark forms moved a step back in response, which I have to be honest, made me feel a little safer.

So here we were in an alien place, who knows where in time and space. I'm contained in a purple bubble of energy and three dark cloaked half human forms are standing before me locked in a deadlock of silence. Well I couldn't run, so there was only one thing left to do - communicate! "What do you want with me" I managed to say in a voice that started off okay, but sounded slightly high pitched in my haste to get the words out. "You must stop – or be stopped" came the reply in a bounding hissing voice which seemed to pause over the letter 's' similar to the snake in Disney's 'Jungle Book'. "But stop what?" I said, almost on impulse. "This – everything" he hissed back. "Why? I don't understand – what am I doing that's wrong? Why must I stop?" I replied.

With this the dark figure I felt was the female, rushed towards me with a piercing howl. I barely had time to flinch before I felt it crash into the barrier of energy and saw tendrils of purple energy flash past my flailing arms as the form was repulsed again. I gathered myself and looked back to the dark forms in time to see the attacker reform with the others. Purple flashes of energy still dissipated and evaporated off its form. It didn't look pleased; I could sense their anger was growing at the helplessness of their situation. This in itself made me realise that I wasn't as defenceless as I had thought. For all their efforts, somehow they couldn't hurt me. With these new thoughts came a new confidence and that feeling of confidence seemed to grow within me.

I looked straight into the nonexistent eyes of the main dark form, and took a step forward towards them. Immediately I sensed a terror, as the two flanking forms seemed to startle and rise and they slid back a few steps in retreat. But not the large dark form - it waited as if to show its powerful defiance, then in its own time it gently slid backwards to rejoin the others, it wasn't afraid. Again we had reached a position of stalemate. Although I wanted to run, there was nowhere to run to, and somehow I felt they would have liked that, so reluctantly I stood my ground and stared.

With a small gesture of movement, the large central form spoke, "Man must not know, man must not be." The last word seemed to trail off forever as the words formed meaning in my mind.

"I don't understand, man must not know what?" I replied in the most confident voice I could muster from my now parched lips.

"He must not know what he is and what he can be, he is ours, has always been ours, he must not transgress."

With these words I saw blurred images fill my mind; I saw man throughout the ages fighting each other over land and property. Man killing man, lying and cheating, and above circling high overhead I saw hundreds of these dark cloaked forms flying high, surveying and controlling, wishing and moving man down this destructive path.

It suddenly became clear to me; man has been influenced and controlled like puppets by these dark forms for their own purposes throughout the millennia. I could see and sense them in the imagery of leaders and decision makers down through the ages – they were mainly in the background hovering like semitransparent shadows lurking against the walls and corners. Then the images broke off and faded.

"You see, we have always been here, we are the caretakers of man. You must not tell them, he has no right to know, he is ours." With these words the tall dark form loomed upwards as if trying to impress their power upon me. If I didn't have the energy shield protecting me, this pea-cocking would have worked and I would have run for the hills.

"But tell him what? I still don't understand" I shouted back.

With this, the female dark form turned to its central leader and whispered "He doesn't know" with a long trailing 'w' sound and the element of surprise in its movements. The larger form lurched sideways with a sweeping arc of its arm, with this it sent the female dark form sprawling backwards leaving a clinging trail of dissipating black smoke in its wake. The large dark form then loomed up as its anger erupted, sending its voice screeching through the air as it looked at me with its menacing, shrouded glare.

"Of course he knows, look at him, he's protected."

Great, I thought, now the attention was back on me. I started to feel very small and very alone once again. The three forms now moved forward, spurred on by the simmering anger from the lead dark form. They moved closer to me and the two minion forms flanked instinctively to each side of their master so as to strengthen the intimidating effect – and to be honest, it was working.

"Now – you're going to forget these little explorations you've had, and you're going to stop them. You're not going to share these experiences with anyone – Who would believe you anyway? No one needs to know" hissed the tall dark form as it loomed so close to the protective shield that I could see small tendrils of energy strain to break away, and move towards it.

"Just let us come closer and we can help you get back, help you forget these follies, so you can get on with your life". As it said this, it reached out a dark gnarled limb in a seemingly friendly gesture towards the shield, but not close enough to touch it. It felt as though it lingered there for eons. The dark gnarled outstretched form of a hand enticing me, captivating me with a power of its own. The longer I looked at it, the easier it started to feel to just reach out, grab it and just get this whole thing over and done with. I mean, why me? I didn't sign up for anything or ask to be whisked away through mini wormholes in time and space to duel with strange beings made of darkness. Darkness, the word lingered in my mind for a second. Then with a great speed, it managed to spark some thoughts, and at a lightening pace I had an idea.

I looked up from the ground and into the eyes of the tall dark adversary. I knew what I was doing and would probably only get one chance with this. I feigned a small shrug, a little drop in my shoulders, enough to signify a small act of defeat which I knew he would sense, and then I started to reach for the outstretched dark limb.

Slowly I reached forward, and this time the bubble of protective white light didn't bounce and expand with my fingers. I could see and feel a slight buoyant pressure as my fingertips started to move through the protection into the space beyond. Slowly this was followed by my palm and my wrist moving closely to my forearm, bringing my face so close to the protective shield that I could feel the hair on my face rise to meet the living, moving energy.

Before me the three dark watchers had formed a close bunched unit. The leader, clearly more dominant, almost seemed to glow with anticipation as it too reached further forward, ready to grasp its prey – me!

We were nearly touching. I could feel the force from the creatures move far beyond their actual presence. A cold wave of energy loomed in the air not unlike the sensation you feel when opening an ice cold freezer door on a scorching day.

I saw the leader prepare to move just that little bit further forward, anticipating its intent to grab my outstretched arm., as he did, I launched my attack. With all the speed I could muster from a squatting position, I leapt forward. My aim was to dive at the feet of my three nemeses. As I launched through the air towards them, I closed my eyes and envisaged my chakra points all simultaneously opening, and great beams of coloured intense light piercing the space around me in a kaleidoscope of rainbow hues.

I hit the floor with a thud that forced me to open my eyes, and in doing so I saw the dark forms lurch trying to find me as I span underneath them. But for them it was too late. I had managed to pull my protective form with me and as I propelled forward at speed and expanded and empowered the force, it had crashed into the dark forms. It moved over them, crackling as it moved causing the dark ones to arch and throw their limbs in wild movements as the walls of my protective shield encased them.

I jumped up from my crumpled position to the feet of the dark forms waiting for an impending attack, but was shocked and relieved to see the idea had worked. There before me I could now clearly see the energy bubble of protection, its curved shape and energy glistening and moving like a ball of water.

Inside, from behind the ripples of vibrating energy, I could see and hear the dark forms as they ricocheted off the walls of the sphere trying to find a way out. Their anger and distress was evident in the piercing cries that were muffled by the walls of the sphere, like voices under water.

I have to admit I smiled; well it was kind of cool! It had worked, and better than I had thought. I watched for a few seconds, lingering and arrogant at my prisoners. As I did so, I saw what I felt was the dark leader move purposely close to the front of the sphere. His face with no features almost touching the energy that seemed to distort him like images through rippled glass.

"We WILL meet againnnn" it hissed as it searched for me with its cold dark face, and I definitely heard this comment. It was time to go back, back to the relative safety of the physical world. I closed my eyes, calmed my racing mind. Then felt my shoulders drop with relaxation as the ground behind me fell away and I felt the tug of time and space pull me backwards and away.

On waking I felt shakier than usual. The group wanted to share their experiences but I held mine back. I meant no ill and believed that some things, the things that do wander in the darkness of what we do, didn't need me to announce their presence and impact their reality into the travels of others. So I kept quiet and wrote the experience in my travel diary to share with you.

Now when I look back and feel the sensations of those cold, lonely creatures as they looked at me, it's not with a fear of them. Yes they are scary, yes they want something from us, but I also feel they are jealous of man, jealous of what we have, the many gifts bestowed upon us. For the most part though, they are hidden from us by our own making, of course with a little help from them, our 'friends'. But I also sensed their fear. They know that we are coming of age and that man is breaking free of the binds and exploring the frontiers of himself and the universes he inhabits. This is what scares them the most, the prospect of when man is truly free, then where does this leave them?

So if you travel and I hope you do, then keep a healthy mind and a watchful fear and respect for beings like this. Know that they too have a place in the scheme of the universe, and just maybe it's part of our destiny to help them find their place, as others help us find ours.

THINGS TO COME – BALANCE IN EVERYTHING

So divinely is the world organized that every one of us, in our place and time, is in balance with everything else.
- Johann Wolfgang von Goethe (1749 - 1832)

It took me a few weeks of personal questioning to get past the experience of the dark forms. The experience had both a chilling effect, but also filled me with a sense of wonder at the possibilities of what the human soul can do in dimensional space, which I was fast learning was anything.

The weeks had passed and the worse memories were fading. I never shared experiences like this with the group. But looking back now objectively, maybe I should have. I knew Brenda would have taken this all in her stride, but some of the others I just wasn't sure about. I didn't want to be the one to scare anyone off this amazing path of discovery so I didn't share. If any of you who read this travel similar pathways with similar discoveries then I do recommend sharing – it is really the only way forward and in some way I hope to atone for my not sharing at the time by doing so within these pages now.

It was great to be seated back at Brenda's. We had just taken a long summer break to accommodate family and summer commitments. Giving me time to think about my experiences with the dark creatures and to dwell and learn from them. I arrived early and Brenda and I exchanged news about friends, family and of all things psychic and mysterious. I updated Brenda on my Remote Viewing *(that's another story)* and she filled me in on her sons round the world travel exploits and his encounters with caged shark diving in South Africa. It was good to be back, it always felt comfortable. We had known each other for a lot of years now, right back to before Brenda had helped my mother organise my wedding at the age of 21 at the local Spiritualist Church. The same place where I would go on to learn all manners of Psychic methods and techniques, from Brenda herself and many other teachers who moved in and out of the varying circles of people over the next sixteen years of our lives.

So here I was again, snuggled peacefully up against the warmth of the old brown leather sofa – my friend, and ready to rush headlong into the wild west frontier of hyperspace and other dimensions.

I closed my eyes, and in a deep breathe expanded my lungs to their fullest, then exhaled slow and long. With this I instantly felt the well worn pattern of internal relaxation take over and my shoulders dropped what felt like inches with the release of tension – the slip into the ether had begun. Slowly with each breath, the physical world slips away, and the real world of possibilities inches forward from the darkness of my mind.

I remember to run through my protective routine, so I envisage steel spikes shooting from the soles of my feet into the earth deep below me, anchoring me to this time and place, a marker so I won't get lost – out there. I then see a glowing ring of protective energy form around us as our Chakra points open, and radiant living energy dissipates in swirling misty tendrils of light. My energy meets the energy from the other three group sitters and it mixes to form an intense spiralling thin band of luminous energy that glowed and buzzed behind us, circling and protecting us from bad in any form, be it intent, physical or purely dimensional.

I vaguely hear Brenda in the space before me – but now she sounds so distant "Now see the portal of light create in the centre of the circle, see it move upwards and outwards into the cosmos". With these words and a shift of our intent, a living pillar of luminous energy forms in between us. This part to me always feels magical. I take great pride and pleasure in watching it form and grow from our energy and then from itself as it becomes a kind of living structure. Within its form which looks like blue, purple and white energy mixed in long streaks; I can see small sparkles of light twist and move as if carried upwards by some flow or stream. The whole energy portal shimmers like the heat from a bonfire on a dark night, and beyond the shimmer I can just make out the relaxed, silent forms of the other members as if they are turned to stone.

I feel myself move forward. I have no weight now and movement feels beautiful, graceful and unhindered, and unlike the physical body where I sometimes have to drag a part of me to start moving, the mere thought of moving starts you moving when out of body.

I approach the light. As I do I feel it buzz, and as I approach a reaction takes place whereby I also buzz. I can feel it all over my form not unlike the sensation of hairs rising on the back of your neck. This is, I feel, where the energy of the portal and the energy that is me start to meet and adjust to each other. As I move forward, this dissipates and I feel myself enter the column of light and am absorbed into a soft warm glow. I look around but all I see are streaks of pulsing light and a white and purple haze. I feel a rumble, slight at first but it grows faster and louder like an approaching train, and then with an expected whoosh I'm propelled upwards at great speed.

Unlike other journeys this was short. I hardly had time to enjoy the tumbling sensation as I travelled through the spiral wormhole appendage watching time and space blur by like a cosmic firework display of magnificent proportions.

Suddenly it just stopped. Wowed by this I looked around and was awed to see nothing around me but the darkness of space. For a few seconds I have to say I freaked out at this situation and until you fully experience a sensation of total space around you with no way of placing yourself within that space, you won't really experience the panic that rushed through me. The overall feeling can I guess be equated to suddenly waking from a dream and finding yourself in the middle of an ocean with nothing else visible, just you and the overbearing space as you tread water. Well now you know what I felt like and funnily enough my limbs were moving in the same action as if I was trying to tread water as I panicked in this space, this freedom.

It didn't take long for the waves of fear to disperse and as they did I found through a little experimentation that I could, by thinking about it, spin and move myself around. As I did I span around and below me was the glowing crescent shaped globe of the Earth below me like some bloated spinning Christmas tree bauble. So magnificent and proud, blue and glowing in the overpowering darkness of space. I remained there just taking in this awesome spectacle of our own planet as it gyrated below me. What made me laugh was that it looked bloated around the middle like it had eaten too many Sunday lunches and it was now straining under its own weight. I guess now when I look back on this experience – it probably is straining.

What held my gaze the most was the light the Earth seemed to radiate like a great big homing beacon in the darkness. Could this be the reason we have UFO's and visitors? Could it be the light that attracts them I thought as I looked at this beautiful spectacle below me? With these thoughts I felt a presence and with panicked movements, remembering my last dimensional encounter, looked around, which is quite hard to do when floating in hyperspace somewhere, because here there are more directions to look in. Behind me I found what I was looking for. There, sitting cross legged as if perched on some invisible chair was a being made of light. At first I squinted, the light from this life form was so bright and shimmering against the dark intensity of the coldness of space behind it. As my nonphysical eyes adapted to the vision, they opened fully and I could see the form in more detail. The form looked feminine in its stature. It didn't have recognisable female body parts or shape, but it just looked feminine, slim and graceful. The form was made of an intense light that seemed to move through pathways around its form not unlike blood vessels carrying blood. But these vessels moved energy, which made the form radiate and catch the light throwing off small rainbow like sparkles. The face had no features, and looked a little like a blank canvas, like an artist had started the painting but hadn't moved onto the face yet. Within the form I could just make out at the key points where we have been told the Chakra points lie, coloured shapes of energy that were slowly rotating. Pumping coloured energy at key points into the tubes carrying the light around its body. The heart seemed to be the largest and this could be seen throwing out a pink glow as the energy radiated outwards through the vessels around its form.

As I breathed in every detail of this beautiful life form it softly lifted its right arm and with its long nimble looking fingers it motioned for me to move closer. Hesitantly I inched nearer with my thoughts till I was about six feet from this angelic looking form. I was just thinking to myself 'this must be an Angel – but where are the wings?' when I hear a sweet gentle laugh, and a smooth reassuring female voice. "No, I'm not an Angel; I'm a friend and teacher." With this, the form motioned and gestured with its head that seemed to synchronise with the words, but they didn't come out of a mouth. "There is much that needs to be said and we don't have much time, so please come closer." Sure, now that I had nothing to fear from the form, I could do nothing but inch yet closer. As I did so I could feel the radiance of the light. It felt like little pin pricks of warmth on the parts of me that faced the form from about four feet away. The energy lines running through the form could now be seen clearly. Like iridescent beads of water and light continuously moving through the body, flowing like blood.

"Yes it is a little like blood – and like blood we also need these energy channels to work correctly and supply the parts of the body, for the body to work and survive. What you see here now in me is also mirrored within all man. It's what connects us to the essence. And the essence is who and what I am."

"So what you're telling me is that you are made up of energy and light?" I said.

"What I'm telling you is that we are ALL made of energy and light. And what you see here within me, moves and lives within you also. There is no difference between us and the worlds we move in, as you have discovered in your travels."

"You said you were the essence, is that your name?" I asked.

"No, I haven't needed an individual name for a long time. It's a description of where I come from, and of where you belong."

"Me? Where I belong?" I gasped, a little awed by this situation. With a voice that sounded like she was smiling came her reply "Not you individually, but man as a whole. We have watched and helped your group and many others on the pathway to a full discovery of who you are and how you fit into the universe. Many times we have wanted to cradle each of you and comfort you in your yearning, to let you know that you are not alone in the universe. You're all part of the essence of the universe and everything has its place within it."

I felt compelled by these words and the tone of her voice that seemed to convey their meaning. I would have loved to have seen my face, I bet my jaw was wide open catching stars as I listened and tried to remember it all.

"I now have some concepts I need you to listen too. When the time is right we want you to tell others, spread the ideas like seeds to the wind, then over time we will ALL see the fruits germinate and spread." "Uh Ok." I half muttered in surprise and confusion. "Man is a reflection of the larger workings of the universe. Within each man is the constant struggle that pervades everything we see and know. The universe is bound by this unwritten law, its fabric entwines and moves everything within the universe, the ebb and flow of the universe depends on this titanic battle. This force you call balance.

Man is the micro version of balance of the universe in play. Within each man there is a lifelong struggle with a multitude of problems and solutions all based around differing forms of balance. This has been reflected in your philosophy, stories, and your entire civilisation since man created his first thoughts. The entire planet is also a larger version of this cosmic struggle between the positive and negative forces of the universe, and at this current moment in time, on one level the balance has clearly shifted off centre in the negative direction, and the living earth battles with you, its inhabitants to try and shift this balance back. There are too many of you, doing too much, with no counter balancing actions, so a balance marker has shifted and this brings a time of turmoil. On a spiritual level man is also in a state of turmoil. Part of man has glimpsed the beauty and truth of spiritual attainment and man's true place within this. At the same time the eternal struggle of shifting balance calls for a reaction to keep the balance. So as people attain what you call the higher spiritual levels a universal balance is also kept with an equal number of human atrocities and negative actions as the balance swings between positive and negative."

Talk about mind blowing, but as the form said these words to me, visions entered my mind. I clearly saw the ancient symbol of Ying & Yang as it cradled the planet. I saw it rock back and forth, swaying from positive to negative, both fighting but ultimately the universe trying to keep the balance between both.

"So what you're saying is – that the more spiritual we become – the more pain we will also see in the world?" I said to the form in a strange moment of clarity at the vision I had seen.

"Correct, but do not feel bad – there is no blame. It's the way of the universe. All creation from the essence is part of unfolding layers of balance. Everything is in a constant struggle. Everything in the universe has choices of which direction to take, and each of these choices and directions impacts upon every other. Envision it if you can – it's like pebbles thrown into a lake. Each stone creates a set of expanding waves that move outwards. Cast a second stone and you get a second set of waves. Where the waves meet you get a conflict, an area where balance makes a choice. Now that we are here let's discuss waves. The universe and you yourself is completely made up of waves. The expanding rhythmic patterns of waves and how they interact with all other waves creates reality, time and space. Of course within this space is YOU. You are made of waves. Man has always had an affinity with waves but the true meaning of this until now has escaped you. How many times has man looked at the sea in wonder or gazed longingly at the movement of the skies. This is a distant memory of the knowledge that was lost. Waves. This is both the answer and the question."

The form seemed to radiate a smile as it finished these words. I could feel an excitement in its movements and the expression of the words. I sensed pride like the pride a parent has for a child when it sees him learn a new skill. I was the child.

I was blinded by the mass of information – I started to grasp an idea of what was being told to me, but somehow it didn't quite sink in. The form sensed this struggle within me and without saying a word leant towards me extending its arm. Before I had any chance to react, the gap between us had evaporated and the long slender finger of the form reached for my brow. I could clearly see iridescent sparkles of light flitter through the translucent light skin of the form, then it touched me.

Things to Come – Balance in Everything

An immense flash of white filled the vision behind my eyes and this opened up to a large vision of a tree in my mind. I could hear the gentle rustle of the leaves like sweet brushing sounds of a green living ocean. I could see the tree almost lurch as its form, its branches and everything about it moved back and forth in a natural rhythm. Instantly and with a jolt, the vision propelled me forward into the tree, through and into a leaf. I could feel the fibres rip and see the differing layers as I propelled deeper into the leaf. I moved way past any describable shapes, images blurred into colours as I moved deeper and deeper into a minute level, but also a level that felt as large as the space above the earth. Approaching fast from in front of me I could see small spheres of dancing light and hear a buzzing noise that grew as we approached. I stopped and seemed to hang in the air in front of these living sparkles of light. Animated and jittery, they seemed to erratically move and flitter from one place to the next, sometimes slow and other times moving like the speed of light and then stopping dead. As I watched I could see that even here, on this deep minute level, the smallest of things were moving in the same way as I had seen the tree move, as the sparkles swayed almost dancing with each other. Then from the right and almost hitting me, in sped another light particle. Bluer than the rest it looped around the others, which seemed to react to it and another intense little dance began. After a few spectacular seconds the sparkles seemed to disperse leaving the blue arrival bouncing like a ball on the ocean in front of me. Before I had time to think, the vision hurtled forward, absorbing me right into the blue orb splintering flashes of light all through my mind. When the light dimmed I could see blurred lines, shapes and forms speed past, nothing recognisable everything a blur like a hyper speed rollercoaster. Finally with a feeling like a pop, I felt we had travelled out of the blue sparkle and when the vision pulled back I was filled with a sense of stunned awe as I could see myself before me. I had travelled inside a leaf and ended up inside myself.

The picture started to dim from my mind. As it did, I could see the fingers of the light form pull back from my face. "You see you are part of the essence, part of the universe, part of everything. You are part of the cosmic motion and the waves you see mirrored in existence all around you are just mirror images of the universe at large. There are three lessons we want you to take away and share, these are: Whatever, however, and whoever, ultimately everything in the universe moves in a movement towards balance. Sometimes a shift in either direction occurs, but balance will always be sought.

Secondly, look towards the natural motion of the universe. Waves can set you free, they are the answer to many of man's dreams, desires and needs.

Thirdly, you are not alone, you ALL have the power to be anything, anywhere and at any time in the universe. As with everything YOU are the essence.

I must go now, a lot has been said and it's time for you to also return to your companions. One more thing, share these insights, it's time for man to know his place. Thank you and safe journeys."

With this the light form raised its right arm, palm faced towards me, and as it did so I could again feel the radiance of a warm smile from its face. Slowly I saw the light form start to fade before me and within seconds all that remained was a small pink spark of light like a floating ember from a fire, and then this too faded.

It seemed cold again without the light from my companion. The darkness quickly fell upon my shoulders and seemed to creep in from all sides as loneliness crept upon me. Luckily this wouldn't last long as I could feel the pulling warp of space around me as everything stretched backwards, propelling me back home at great speed to the physical world.

A NEW WORLD

Ideals are like stars: you will not succeed in touching them with your hands, but like the seafaring man on the ocean desert of waters, you choose them as your guides, and following them, you reach your destiny.
*- **Carl Schurz** (1829 - 1906)*

Where do you go after an experience like that? You wake up from one day to another and look around but something's changed. People still mill around with silent dazed looks as they file to work in the early morning throng. But something's different, then you realise it's YOU.

The days after this series of encounters passed in a daze to me. Then like a drunk slowly rising from a year long stupor, the numbness starts to fade and the mind starts to absorb the impact of what you have learnt.

Now that I can look back on the experience with a clear, objective mind I realise it's not unlike an awakening. An awakening of the soul, a realisation that there are no boundaries to what man can do, with no boundaries to where we can go. Man has been asking the questions about the meaning of life, and looking for life in the farthest reaches of the galaxy, but at the same time he has ignored the yearning, niggling feeling that resides within us all. This universal knowing that there is more! And there is, it's been there all along waiting for us – we just need to stop, to take a deep breath, to shut out the noisy complicated world we have created. It's only then when we can truly reflect inwards that we can move outwards and grow into the beings we are destined to be.

I know now that the universe is filled with beautiful and varied life. That other worlds and dimensions exist in the smallest of places and that we as human beings are special and that we have access to them all. I also now know that as in everything there are misguided dark souls who seem to upset the universal balance out of a selfish greed for themselves. As you have read I have personally battled some of them and still on occasion catch myself thinking back to their chilling message that we will meet again, and we probably will. A part of me excitedly waits for this time, for armed with the knowledge that we are both creators of our own destiny and the universes around us.

When you start your psychic travels you too may meet beings like these. On the other hand you may not, its huge out there and each and every one of us has a different road to travel. One thing is sure wherever you go and however you psychically travel, beings of immense knowledge, light and love await to guide you on your journey.

My journey hasn't ended. I see that it has only just begun. This book represents a small handful of my psychic experiences in these hidden realms that reside just a blink away. It's now up to you to add your experiences to mine.

If you take anything from my experiences, I hope it's YOUR journey and a start of YOUR movement towards knowing. As the life forms have shared with me, life and the universe exist around balance in all things and a movement in waves. I hope that you can leap on your surf board at the top of this crest of a wave – ride this information out, and surf the psychic internet to find YOUR truth, and YOUR true self, YOUR destiny. It's all out there waiting for you!

YOU CAN TRAVEL THE PSYCHIC INTERNET

"When we raise ourselves through meditation to what unites us with the spirit, we quicken something within us that is eternal and unlimited by birth and death
Once we have experienced this eternal part in us, we can no longer doubt its existence. Meditation is thus the way to knowing and beholding the eternal, indestructible, essential centre of our being."

- Rudolf Steiner

You too can travel the psychic internet and experience your own explorations, just like the ones I describe in this book - or even better!

Its part of man's hidden destiny to use these inbuilt powers, it's not just for a psychic few, but with a little practice it's available to all. Within these next few chapters we move you through some of the basic tools and practices that will allow you to start developing your own pathway. As you develop, you may develop new and different skills and methods of your own. This is OK! It's a natural progression, we are all different and different things work for us all. For example when psychic travelling alone I like to listen to music. When psychic travelling in a group the other members might not like music and feel it's a distraction. We are all different; there is no set way to accomplish this freedom it's an intuitive skill.

Use these presented methods as your initial basis for discovery, expand them, change them and explore.

MEDITATION

What is meditation?

There are many types of meditation developed and used in every corner of the world. Traditionally meditation was (and still is) used for spiritual growth...i.e. becoming more conscious of our inner selves; unfolding our inner Light, Love, & Wisdom; becoming more aware of a guiding Presence in our lives. More recently, meditation has become a valuable tool for finding a peaceful oasis of relaxation and in a demanding, fast-paced world. The one definition that fits almost all forms of meditation is... 'consciously directing your attention to alter your state of consciousness.' Another way of putting it is 'conscious relaxation.'

The use of meditation for healing is not new. Meditative techniques are the products of diverse cultures and it is rooted in the traditions of the world's religions. Nearly all the religious forms practice meditation in one form or another. The knowledge that meditation can promote healing has been known and passed down for thousands of years. The benefits of meditation include psychical healing, emotional healing, and extending concentration, finding inner peace, guidance, insight and a tool for exploring other realities.

When one starts to use meditation in their lives it opens up many doorways. On its own it's an invaluable tool to escape the technological, fast paced world that is expanding around us, which is sometimes frightening but always demanding and stressful. When combined with an exploratory conscious direction, meditation can be the doorway to new worlds like the physical Stargate in the film/TV series. Every time they travelled through the Stargate they entered a new world – and with basic meditation, so can you. With time and commitment to the process, meditation becomes the doorway to these new worlds and experiences and also the doorway to your true self.

How do I meditate?

Learning to meditate is easier than you might imagine. Most of us in our daily lives have used the core practices of meditation techniques to get us through the day. Maybe during aerobics or sports training, when we concentrate and focus on getting past the pain to the goal, or when you visit the dentist and you pick a spot on the ceiling, concentrate hard and try to get your mind to think of something else.

Breathing

One of the best and well used techniques for meditation is 'breathing focus'. By making the practical effort to focus completely on the way we breathe and how the breath comes in and out of the body, we take our minds away from the background noise that swallows us in our everyday lives. The rhythmic pattern of the body and how we breathe creates a perfect tool for meditation.

What will happen to me?

With a little time and effort you will experience the state I call 'separation'. Within this state the mind is crystal clear and empty. There is no background noise, there are no everyday stresses and problems, and in the best cases there is even no sensation of your physical body. Within this state I feel crystal clear, for me it's like being in a warm, dark soundproof room. I can, if I concentrate still hear the outside world but it's distant and muffled, not part of where I am, in the moment.

HOW TO EXPLORE THE PSYCHIC INTERNET.

This section is divided into the basic guidelines needed for using meditation to explore the psychic internet. They are in no way the only way to do this, and if you feel that there are elements you want to change and that you feel will suit you better, then try them.

INTENT

Before you travel, and in fact before you start this entire process, take some time to think about where you want to go, some of the things you would like to see or achieve. Try to use this as a mental key for the journey, or as a roadmap. This could be a question you need an answer to, a place you've always thought about, or just the intent to meet new beings and to develop yourself. This intent may be the driving force that opens up doorways to new experiences. Sometimes good and sometimes bad – to test us, to move us forward. It is possible to just go with the flow and see where the universe wants to take you, but other times you may need a pathway and your intent will forge this pathway for you.

YOU

As you are the main proponent to psychic exploration, it's important to create the best possible opportunities for travel to happen. For this to happen clothing needs to be comfortable and loose fitting. It helps if you have recently used the toilet and also if you are not either full of food or feeling hungry. A glass of water is handy during the meditation which helps in case of dryness. Before you start the actual process try to get in the frame of mind of calming down, relaxing and slowly making the real world dissipate into the background. I do this by creating a large old suitcase in my mind's eye, I open the case and inside I throw all the worries from the day and my life. In goes that niggling work problem, money, the bills, and whatever may be floating around. I then close the lid and slide the case to one side, allowing me to concentrate on the one thing ahead, travel.

YOUR TOOLS

These generally encompass a glass of water in case of thirst. A pen and paper, a good flowing pen is advisable. At key points during or after the meditation it's important to record the observations. This will allow for an accurate record of your travels as well as a great resource and confirmation tool with any other group members and for recording any premonitions or elements, facts or details that need to be researched.

POSITION

Overall you will need to find a quiet comfortable place to meditate. Eliminate as much noise and distraction as possible. This generally involves sitting comfortably in a chair. Other forms of meditation with other goals allow any comfortable position; on the bed, floor, sitting, lying, cross-legged or whatever feels right. If working in a small group, then position the chairs in a circular position creating a ring or circle. This positioning has a two-fold purpose. Firstly it's the recognized shape and symbol created when protecting oneself when involved in psychic work. Secondly its form helps in the movement of subtle energies that are created by the meditative states. An adept practitioner can readily see the movement and flow of this energy around the group members during a session. The overall body position for meditation should be relaxed with your spine reasonably straight. Your hands should be relaxed and placed in a position which is comfortable for you. Your pen and paper must be nearby for when you need them, but also not in the way of your relaxing objectives. The feet are generally placed in a comfortable position with both feet planted flat on the floor. To help the flow of energy through the body we tend to position our arms and legs so they do not cross. Once you have achieved a similar position, you are ready to start.

PROTECTION AND GROUNDING

I come from a background of classical psychic training, therefore as taught in this time old way, I like to protect myself with a shell of white energy. The universe is a vast complex beast and as with all things there are good and bad life forms. For this reason you need a protective field around you to discourage the bad. This field is created by you from your internal energy and expanded around yourself. This field I envision as a ball of intense white light that forms outwards from my heart Chakra. As it moves out in front of me I envision it spreading outwards as it forms a field of living energy around me. As the energy shield is created I enforce the terms of the shield 'nothing dark or evil shall intrude upon me or near me through this shield – all good may approach and enter but all that is bad will rebound in terror and fear.' This is my form of protection based on my teachings and experience, if you have one of your own, then use this, there are no rules. If this is your first foray into these realms then do as I do – imagine a protective white energy barrier surrounds you repelling the bad and embracing the good. This should work for you but if you feel you need to know more, then there are excellent books on the subject like the timeless book *Psychic Self Defense* by Dion Fortune, *ISBN: 1578631513.*

Next comes the grounding. Again another throwback from my classical training, it's a procedure that is meant to always allow you to successfully travel back home. This is an anchor to this time and place so however deep you go into hyperspace, you will always have a way back home. This exercise comprises of envisioning tendrils or roots sprouting out from your feet like a plant down deep into the ground and earth below you, until you feel securely fastened in place. If done successfully, your feet should feel heavy and fastened in place for your journey.

BREATHING & RELAXING

Now you are almost ready! You close your eyes, relax your shoulders and take your first deep breath and exhale very slowly. As you exhale you should feel your shoulders loosen, and one by one you start to relax the physical body to the rhythm of the breathing. My process of this works from the feet to the head. I breathe in and think of my feet. When I breathe out I envision my feet relaxing and all the stress and strain from the day is carried away with the breath. I then repeat the same process for my knees, thighs, groin, stomach, chest, shoulders, arms, neck and finally my head. By this stage the actual breathing rhythm has slowed and I am fully relaxed. The body should be totally relaxed, so take a second and scan your body from head to foot and if you find an area not relaxed then repeat the process until it is. You know when this stage has been fully achieved when you can still feel your body, but if feels whole, a single relaxed and unified form, lighter than usual and slightly distant.

THE DOORWAY

If working in a group or by yourself, envision a stream of energy separating from you. Feel it form from your life force and the natural energy created by the meditation. See this energy move through the air like a wispy cloud until it sits about four feet away, or if in a group, it sits in the middle of the circle. See this energy take shape, expand and grow as you continue to feed it. Watch it grow, and as it does you can see it twist and rotate in a clockwise direction like a mini tornado of pure subtle energy. After a few minutes you see the energy tunnel expand in height as it reaches for the ceiling up and out into the vast space above. This is your portal. By now this portal you have created is buzzing with the energy that created it. It writhes as it spins inviting you to enter. Take a few minutes to recuperate some of the energy you have used to create it and then visualize yourself entering the portal. When you do you will feel a pulling sensation as the portal pulls you up and out into the vastness of hyperspace and dimensions. You are now on your journey.

COMING HOME

At any point during your travels you can come back just by thinking about returning. This will cause your mind to initiate a process that will pull you back into this dimension and away from wherever you are. If working as a group a pre-determined target time, of say an hour, might be set. This will act as a guide for your internal body clock. Feel yourself slowly pulled back into the physical reality. Little by little feel the sensation return to your limbs and your soul floating back down into the body. Sometimes these processes feel sluggish but stick with it, restart the deep breathing process and with every breath out feel your body start to come back to life and the senses open to the physical world.

CLOSING

Take time to close yourself down. See and feel your grounded roots pull up from the protective earth freeing your feet to move. See the energy that created the portal and the protective shields dissipate and disperse into the air around you. When you feel centered and whole, open your eyes.

TRAVEL DIARIES

A key part of dimensional experiences and travel is recording all that you experience. Sometimes this means pulling out of a session and recording notes then going back into it, or if you have a good memory, waiting until you get back then recording what you have seen and experienced. There is no right or wrong way – it's whatever works best for you and you will only find out which that is by experimenting. When you have finished the note taking, and if you are travelling as a group, it becomes the ideal time to discuss your individual experiences one by one, over a well needed refreshing drink to supplement the energy you have used and lost. Take a few minutes each to summarise what you've experienced, share insights and comments. If you have any predictions, messages or communications, share them with the group. There may be others with similar experiences - it's all about working together.

If you are travelling alone or in a group then feel free to share your experiences at our online website www.surfingthepsychicinternet.com – here you will find resources and other fellow travelers who may have help and adventures to share.

Keep a special notebook for your experiences – I call mine 'my travel diaries' – these hold all the experiences of ten years of travel and communications. Remember to always note the location and date of your experience, then record all that you can remember or that feels relevant. This will also be a great guide to look back on if you get any predictive experiences. Any kind of notebook will do the trick, hard backed is best as finding a writing surface half in and out of meditative states, and in semi darkness can be hard to impossible. Also don't forget a comfortable, flowing pen.

SURFING THE PSYCHIC INTERNET – YOU ARE NOT ALONE!

Go confidently in the direction of your dreams! Live the life you've imagined. As you simplify your life, the laws of the universe will be simpler.
- Henry David Thoreau *(1817 - 1862)*

Don't worry! You are not alone on your journey. I hope that if this book teaches you one thing it's the answer to that question.

If you have any questions or would like to share your journeys and experiences then please do so at; www.surfingthepsyhicinternet.com.

Here you will find FAQ (frequently asked questions), resources, friends, and me! We await YOU and the chance to share and enjoy the experience you make with YOUR psychic journeys.

SUGGESTED WEBSITES / SOURCES:

www.surfingthepsychicinternet.com

Home for this book with community, FAQ's and much more. Visit us explore and share your experience, meet other friends and travelers.

www.livingthefield.com

Lynne McTaggart began work on The Field four years ago as a personal quest to see if any new scientific theories could explain how homeopathy and spiritual healing work. This journey took her to many areas around the globe, meeting with top frontier scientists in Russia, Germany, France, England, South American, Central America and the USA.

www.whatthebleep.com

What the Bleep Do We Know!? has been a wake-up call for millions of people around the world who have been addressing Life's BIG questions: Who are we? Where are we going? What is consciousness? Do we create reality? How do we effect change?

ABOUT THE AUTHOR

Daz Smith has trained in classical psychic skills for most of his life. Including; healing, clairvoyance, mediumship, aura reading and many other forms of classical psychic skills. His skills vastly improve after learning the CIA form of Remote Viewing from an American in London. Through many years of trial and error with Remote Viewing Daz's psychic skills expand opening up new psychic connections.

Brenda an old friend and psychic teacher asks Daz to join a small select group of psychics, and from this point on all of their lives would never be the same again.

Daz currently owns and manages two paranormal websites. www.crowdedskies.com – a website about aliens and UFO's & www.remoteviewed.com – a website detailing and presenting Remote Viewing with manuals, official CIA documents and real Remote Viewing examples.

Daz currently lives in Bath, in the U.K with his wife Debra and their son Brandon.